Clinical
Social
Work

SAGE SOURCEBOOKS FOR THE HUMAN SERVICES SERIES

Series Editors: ARMAND LAUFFER and CHARLES GARVIN

Recent Volumes in this Series

Mary Nomme Russell

Clinical
Social
Work

Research and Practice

SAGE SOURCEBOOKS FOR THE HUMAN SERVICES SERIES 14

SAGE PUBLICATIONS
The International Professional Publishers
Newbury Park London New Delhi

10-19-95

For information address:

SAGE Publications, Inc.
2455 Teller Road
Newbury Park, California 91320

SAGE Publications Ltd.
6 Bonhill Street
London EC2A 4PU
United Kingdom

SAGE Publications India Pvt. Ltd.
M-32 Market
Greater Kailash I
New Delhi 110 048 India

Printed in the United States of America

Library of Congress Cataloging-in-Publication Data

Russell, Mary Nomme.
    Clinical social work : research and practice / by Mary Nomme Russell.
        p.   cm. -- (Sage sourcebooks for the human services series : v. 14)
    Includes bibliographical references and index.
    ISBN 0-8039-3782-2 (C). -- ISBN 0-8039-3783-0 (P)
    1. Psychiatric social work—United States. 2. Medical social work—United States. I. Title. II. Series.
HV690.U6R87 1990
362.1'0425--dc20   90-39523
                                                                          CIP

FIRST PRINTING, 1990

Sage Production Editor: Judith L. Hunter

CONTENTS

PREFACE

The aim of this book is to provide a review of the research in clinical social work from 1970 to 1988. Given the wealth of study of clinical process in social work over the past two decades, such a review is necessary to integrate and summarize findings. It is only by providing such reviews that a sound empirical base for clinical practice can be established. Reviews of research in social work have been few in number, compared to other disciplines, and none has heretofore provided a comprehensive review of clinical studies. Furthermore, only limited reviews of research in the 1970s and 1980s have been available. The present review, by including 18 years of research published in 11 major social work journals, provides an extensive and comprehensive overview that can benefit both clinical social work practitioners and researchers.

Clinical social workers striving to improve their practice can benefit from empirical study of the clinical process. By attempting to determine what types of interventions are best suited to particular types of clients and/or problems, empirical research has provided clinicians with useful insights. Furthermore, clinical research has aided in the development and improvement of clinical assessment methods as well as provided data about and methods for evaluation of practice.

Social workers engaged in clinical research require an understanding of prior research on which to base and develop further studies. Previous studies not only serve to indicate what types of questions have been asked but also raise questions for further study. In presenting summaries of aims, methods, and results of previous inquiry, reviews provide the necessary background and grounding of future studies.

Chapter 1

RESEARCH AND CLINICAL SOCIAL WORK

Clinical social work has become the most frequent description of social work positions available in job postings in the past decade (Billups & Julia, 1987). The dramatic increase in the use of the term clinical social work reflects significant gains in the acceptance and status of this designation. Several factors have been instrumental in altering initial suspicions that it was elitist, biased toward psychopathology, and unmindful of the social origins of the social work profession. Influences that have operated to allay these concerns have included social legislation, the demands of the marketplace, and developments within social work organizations.

Social legislation has been enacted that makes social workers accountable not only to their own professional organizations, but to society at large. Legislation providing licensure for social work practitioners has resulted in legally enforceable professional standards (Kutchins & Kirk, 1987). The marketplace for clinical psychosocial services has expanded, as have opportunities for autonomous social work practice. Substantial growth in private practice, fostered by the opportunity of direct third-party billing, has been observed among social workers (Shatkin, Frisman, & McGuire, 1986). Clinical social work organizations have been founded, and a substantial clinical social work literature including journals and texts has developed. These professional developments have been expanded further through educational programs specifically designed to produce experts in clinical practice (Pharis & Williams, 1984). The net result has been the emergence within the profession of a well-defined clinical social work identity with its own body of developing knowledge.

Clinical research in social work has been instrumental in advancing clinical practice. Research has helped to clarify the definition of clinical social work, has provided direction in refining the essential elements of clinical practice, and has been used to determine both the effectiveness and the efficiency of clinical interventions. In the health field, for example, improvements in social work status, clinical involvement, and criteria for practice have been attributed directly to clinical research by social workers (Coulton, 1985; Rehr, 1984; Reinherz, Grob, & Berkman, 1983). The effects of clinical research on clinical practice have been dramatic, in many ways outstripping Reid's (1974) projections regarding the use of information systems, field experimentation, and empirical practice models, all of which seemed revolutionary at the time.

The union of clinical research and practice, however, has not been without inherent tensions. These tensions, to some degree, have been due to misperceptions about the nature of clinical practice and clinical research. Clinical practitioners have viewed with some suspicion demands by researchers for rigor and specificity in definitions of practice-related concepts, fearing that simple, explicit definitions would fail to capture the complexity of clinical interactions. Likewise, clinicians have resisted research requirements for uniformity in implementation of clinical interventions on the grounds that it fails to consider changing client concerns and problems. Clinicians have questioned the adequacy of measures used by researchers to evaluate outcome and the utility of studying increasingly narrow and selective aspects of clinical interventions. Clinicians have suggested that researchers who increasingly focus on precisely defined and delimited aspects of clinical interventions risk missing a more fundamental and comprehensive understanding of the whole.

Clinical researchers, in turn, have been frustrated by amorphous and loosely defined clinical language, which is difficult to pin down and operationalize. Researchers also have found it difficult to assess mutable and intuitive approaches to intervention, which are not consistently applied across cases or situations. Researchers further have despaired over clinicians' failure to assess outcome with standardized, reliable, and valid outcome indicators.

In spite of these inherent tensions between research and practice, clinical social work has been increasingly influenced by research methods and results (Bloom & Fischer, 1982; Jayaratne & Levy, 1979). Similarly clinical researchers have become increasingly aware of the need for collaboration with practitioners, recognizing that the value of clinical research is dependent on adequate conceptualization of clinical practice (Saari, 1987). A clear definition of clinical social work, therefore, is essential to the study of the process.

DEFINITION OF CLINICAL SOCIAL WORK

The definition of clinical social work approved and legitimized by the National Association of Social Workers (NASW) states that it is "the professional application of social work theory and methods to the treatment and prevention of psychosocial dysfunctions, disability or impairment, including emotional and mental disorders . . . and includes interventions directed to interpersonal interactions, intrapsychic dynamics and life support and management issues. . . . The perspective of person-in-situation is central to clinical social work practice" (Clinical Social Work Council, 1984). More specifically, Ewalt (1979) stated that clinical social work involved facilitating change among individuals, couples, and small groups, without excluding the possibility of interventions with larger social systems. Goldstein (1979) reiterated that clinical social workers are primarily "people helpers" as opposed to "society changers."

The centrality of the person-in-situation perspective has been described as the sine qua non of social work and the attribute that demarcates it from other clinical disciplines (Cohen, 1979; Dorfman, 1988). Psychotherapeutic activity has been considered part of, but not the whole of, clinical social work, leading to a condensed definition of clinical social work as "psychotherapy plus" (Hollis, 1972). The emphasis on both psychological and social forces in clinical assessment and intervention has been mirrored in clinical social work research, which encompasses the study of intrapersonal, interpersonal, and social factors in the clinical process.

Pluralism or eclecticism in practice, while not part of the definition of clinical social work, has been the observed nature of clinical practice (Jayaratne, 1982). This eclecticism in clinical methods, although providing flexibility of approach, in turn has required informed decision-making regarding appropriate interventions in particular situations. Clinical research hence has investigated which clients with what problems in what kinds of situations require what types of interventions provided by what kinds of clinicians (Strupp, 1978). This kind of empirical base has increasingly been considered a necessary part of clinical practice (Bloom & Fischer, 1982; Jayaratne & Levy, 1979).

Evaluation of practice, as a means of providing accountability, has likewise been increasingly considered an essential element of clinical social work (Lurie, 1979; Rehr, 1984). Professional accountability, whereby clinicians were accountable to clients and monitored within the profession by supervisors and administrators, has been superseded by demands for legal and fiscal accountability to authorities outside the profession. Clinical social workers have been held legally responsible for demonstrating that they have utilized the level of care and skill expected of a reasonably competent practitioner acting in a similar manner under the same or similar circumstances. Malpractice litigation has been instigated against social workers who have been perceived as failing to meet this standard (Kutchins & Kirk, 1987). Fiscal accountability has been demanded of clinicians by increasingly cost-conscious health and welfare administrators, who demand that social workers provide services that are not only clinically effective but also cost-effective (Rehr, 1984). Evaluation of practice, therefore, no longer is simply a laudable goal; increasingly, it is a necessity of clinical practice.

In view of the fact that clinical research, while not part of the definition of clinical social work is nevertheless an essential counterpart to practice, an understanding of the empirical base of clinical practice is necessary. The present review attempts to provide such a base. Before proceeding to the review, however, an understanding of the nature of clinical research in social work is necessary.

DEFINITION OF CLINICAL RESEARCH

Berg and Smith (1985) proposed a description of clinical research that stressed the centrality of research relationships and the impact of these relationships on the investigative process. Modifying this definition to make it specific to social work, clinical research can be defined as *the intensive, involved investigation, including self-scrutiny, taking place predominantly in clinical settings, of clinical processes including all participants and their social contexts.*

In this definition, intensity of investigation refers to the small-scale, in-depth study that is required to understand the highly variable interactions and dynamics within the clinical process. Generalizations that ensue from replication rather than from large-scale investigation tend to be the rule.

Involvement in investigation refers to the researchers' experience with clinical practice, which is necessary to develop meaningful questions for investigation. Marsh (1983) described the historical commitment of pioneer social workers to combining practice and research. Pieper (1985), commenting on contemporary social work research, noted the need to consider researcher-subject relationships and the need to appreciate the complexity of these relationships in research. Involvement also refers to the researcher's responsibility for all aspects of the research process.

Self-scrutiny in clinical research includes the necessity of researcher sensitivity to the sociopolitical contexts in which research takes place and willingness to examine personal and structural forces that influence research. An example of this is the treatment of the sexes in research (Eichler, 1988).

The locale of clinical investigation has primarily, but not exclusively, been clinical settings. Analogue research, in which clinical relationships are simulated in written descriptions or in role plays, have provided useful clinical data in numerous social work studies. Social work studies furthermore have focused on participants, in processes as well as social contexts. Subjects, investigated within each of these areas are outlined later in this chapter.

A further element in the definition of social work research was added by Jayaratne and Levy (1979), who suggested that clinical social work research must meet the criterion of utility. In their opinion, clinical data collected without systematic and continuous analysis for clinical decision-making purposes serves a very limited function. Bloom and Fischer (1982) noted further that the search for clinically useful information is a continuous process, and, therefore, clinical research requires a commitment to keep searching for new and more effective clinical interventions.

Inasmuch as the goals of clinical research and clinical practice can be perceived as complementary and overlapping, the notion of the integration of research and practice has developed in clinical social work. A number of models of integration have been developed.

INTEGRATION OF RESEARCH AND PRACTICE

Many different terms, such as "scientist-practitioner" and "practitioner-researcher," have been used in the social work literature to denote the ideal of practice-research integration (Barlow, Hayes, & Nelson, 1984; Bloom & Fischer, 1982; Jayaratne & Levy, 1979). Although these terms have been used primarily in relation to single-subject designs, they also apply to the broader notions of clinical practitioners making clinical decisions based on empirical data and systematically evaluating their clinical processes and outcomes (Ivanoff, Blythe, & Briar, 1987).

Empirically based decision-making was the central component of the BESDAS model of effective practice described by Thomas (1977). The six components of the model, the first letters of which comprise the acronym, were the use of behavioral targets, empirically based knowledge, specific intervention procedures, data-guided practice, accountable outcomes, and self-correcting practice. Through the use of these components, which require using both research methods and research knowledge, it was expected that clinical practice could be improved. Furthermore, it was suggested that clinical decision-makers could access the available data base through computers (Gibbs & Johnson, 1983). While this ideal model of practice-research integration has been promoted in professional education and in the social work literature, studies of the implementation of such integration have reported mixed results.

RESEARCH UTILIZATION BY SOCIAL WORKERS

Studies on social workers' research utilization have varied in definition of research utilization, the extent to which utilization was linked with specific training, and the type of social workers studied. A 10-year review of surveys yielded research utilization rates ranging from 83% in a small sample of social workers trained in single-case evaluation methods in a supportive agency milieu (Mutschler, 1984) to a low of 8% in a study of social workers with no specified research training who were employed by the military (Cheatham, 1987). The predominant finding in these surveys has been that about one-third of social workers refer to or engage in research as part of their professional activities (Eldridge, 1983; Gingerich, 1984; Kirk & Fischer, 1976; Kirk, Osmalov & Fischer, 1976; Welch, 1983). Somewhat higher rates were reported by specific subgroups of social workers. Pediatric social workers, for example, reported a 57% participation rate (Pfouts & McDaniels, 1977), and behavioral social workers reported a 38% participation rate (Cheatham, 1987). In contrast, a rate of 11% was reported in a study that defined research utilization as practicing evaluative methods provided in training two years post-training (Richey, Blythe, & Berlin, 1987). While it is clear that these rates allow considerable room for improvement, it is not clear whether social workers use research less than other helping professionals or that their utilization rate is unconscionably low, as has been suggested by some reviewers. It is more likely that social workers, like other professionals, use research when the benefits of its utilization are immediate and obvious and the costs of using it are minimal.

Several studies have addressed the issue of perceived obstacles or barriers to research utilization. The most frequently identified barrier to research utilization has been lack of agency demand, support, or reward for its utilization (Gingerich, 1984; Richey, Blythe, & Berlin, 1987; Welch, 1983). The importance of agency support was further demonstrated in Mutschler's (1984) study of six family service workers who were trained and supported in using single-case evaluation. All but one reported integration of evaluation with regular clinical practice at four-month follow-up.

In a multivariate analysis of factors associated with research utilization in a survey of 317 clinicians, Cheatham (1987) found that a positive attitude toward integration of research and practice was the most important factor, followed by the amount and adequacy of training in using evaluative methods and the presence of supportive contingencies within agencies for the systematic evaluation of practice. Although positive attitudes toward research-practice integration are undoubtedly essential, Eldridge (1983b) suggested (on the basis of a survey of 45 mental health social workers) that attitudes alone might not be sufficient. The majority of social workers in this survey professed interest in and expressed verbal support for practice accountability, but only about one-third translated these beliefs into clinical behavior.

Research utilization among clinical social workers has further been constrained by the limited nature of research-based knowledge available. In many areas of social work practice no empirical data base exists (Reid, 1984). Information regarding the effectiveness or appropriateness of different intervention methods is particularly limited (Hanrahan & Reid, 1984). Practical experience, rather than empirical research, continues to be the most frequently used base for practice prescriptions, as revealed in a six-year study of clinical articles by Nurius, Wedenoja, and Tripodi (1987). Although the reasons for clinicians' low reliance on empirical data were not discussed in this study, the lack of clinically relevant information may be partly at fault. Clinical psychology has reported similar deficiencies in basing clinical decisions on inconclusive comparative studies (Lambert, Shapiro, & Bergin, 1986).

Another difficulty in utilizing research data for clinical purposes has been the low level of generalization in social work studies. When valid generalizations cannot be made, it is difficult for practitioners to know when and how to extrapolate research findings to various clinical populations. In a five-year survey of research articles, Nurius and Tripodi (1985) reported that generalization procedures were based primarily on tests of statistical significance with little replication of studies to confirm or extend findings. The authors concluded that the external validity and generalization of the results reported in social work studies was often not at a sufficient level to make studies useful to clinical practitioners. In particular, generalization procedures were lacking in single-case studies, so that clinicians were left with no guidelines to indicate in what situations and with what clients the interventions reported might be successful.

In summary, research utilization by social workers has been of a modest nature and most evident under conditions of agency support and reward. In addition to environmental factors, attitudinal and training factors have been shown to influence the extent of research utilization. Finally, the adequacy of the research itself has had some bearing on the extent of research-practice integration among social workers. All in all, consideration of these limitations has led some social workers to question the appropriateness of a scientific or empirically based approach to practice.

CRITIQUES OF EMPIRICALLY BASED PRACTICE

The assumptions underlying the scientist-practitioner model, namely, that research methods can be utilized by clinical practitioners as part of their practice and that clinical processes are parallel to, if not equivalent to, research processes, have not been accepted unequivocally (Tripodi & Epstein, 1978). Criticism has been wide ranging, encompassing both the nature of social work and the applicability of scientific processes to social work. Peile (1988) noted that these types of concerns have existed since the beginning of social work and are essentially a continuation of the dilemma faced by early social workers in trying to decide whether social work was an art or a science. Peile also noted that the personal, polarized, and at times irrational nature of the debates about these issues suggested that they are more political than scientific. This point had been made earlier by Karger (1983), who suggested that the hidden agenda of the debate was control and power over the future direction of social work.

Critics of the scientist-practitioner or empirical model of practice have stated that these approaches, which tend to be quantitative, logical, linear, and short-term, are likely to become oppressively restrictive, mechanistic, and reductionistic (Siporin, 1985). Saleeby (1979), for example, claimed that empirically based practice was inherently manipulative and was likely to lead to Machiavellian interventions. The preeminence of experimental design and quantitative analyses has also been decried on the basis of its purportedly contrived, potentially oppressive, and masculine nature (Davis, 1985; Heineman, 1981; Ruckdeschel, 1985; Ruckdeschel & Farris, 1981). It has been suggested by critics that attempts to integrate practice with research are likely to produce reductions in standards of both service provision and clinical research (Ivanoff, Blythe, & Berlin, 1987).

Although the debate regarding the benefits of empirically based practice in social work has at times been acrimonious, a number of modifications have been made by each side of the debate. Schuerman (1987) observed that empirical clinicians have conceded that their original aspirations of practice-research integration were overly ambitious. Schuerman suggested that clinical empiricists could and should be involved in development of interventions, as well as in the evaluation of interventions. Peile (1988) noted that the myth of value-free research originally held by some researchers has been replaced by a recognition of the influence of researcher values in clinical studies. Furthermore, the range of methodological options within social work research has been increased in that qualitative as well as quantitative methods have received recognition. Combinations of methods have been advocated by some researchers so that the types of problems investigated could increasingly be matched with different types of data collection and analysis procedures (Geismar & Wood, 1982). Smith (1987), for example, reiterated that outcome research founded on traditional positivist assumptions with specific informational purposes could be used in conjunction with other research approaches founded on different assumptions, using different methods, capable of generating different kinds of information. Witkin (1989) also noted the need for multiple perspectives and methodologies to develop social work knowledge.

Although evidence of the acceptability of diverse methods for obtaining knowledge necessary for clinical practice has increased, the integration and dissemination of this knowledge has not been assiduously promoted. A review of current clinical knowledge developed through social work research has been lacking. Research reviews, which summarize and disseminate diverse research findings, are appropriate vehicles by which to provide busy practitioners with empirically based, practice-related information. Social work research reviews have been published (Maas, 1966, 1971), but these have not been updated nor been specific to clinical practice. Currently, research findings of relevance to clinical social workers are scattered throughout the numerous journals, which have proliferated at an ever increasing rate. A review of current research pertaining to clinical social work was hence deemed in order.

INVESTIGATING THE CLINICAL PROCESS

Scope of Present Review

The present review summarizes research in clinical social work that was published between 1970 and 1988. It is based primarily on clinical research presented in 11 major social work journals that are devoted to research and/or clinical practice. The journals reviewed were *Social Work, Social Casework, Social Service Review, Journal of Social Service Research, Social Work Research & Abstracts, Social Work with Groups, Journal of Social Work Education, Clinical Supervisor, Social Work in Health Care, Health and Social Work,* and *Clinical Social Work Journal.* In addition, journals outside the field of social work and books or monographs, both within and outside social work, were consulted. They provided necessary background for amplification of topics presented in social work journal articles.

The scope of the present review has several acknowledged limitations. Social work research appearing in social work journals other than those listed above was not included. Social work research appearing in journals outside of social work also was excluded. Research presented in doctoral and master's dissertations was not included unless it was presented in a journal article. Books and monographs presenting research findings were only included if they were referred to in journal articles and provided background for and expansion of research findings reported in the journals surveyed. The present review, therefore, cannot be considered to be a comprehensive review of the clinical research literature, but rather an approximation thereof circumscribed by the aforementioned limitations.

The primary criterion for selection of studies in the present review was that they pertain to the practice or application of clinical social work, as opposed to basic research aimed at development of knowledge about social problems. While the latter knowledge is indispensable to the practice of clinical social work, it is beyond the scope of the present review as it encompasses the major part of all social science research. Studies were included in the review only if they involved the collection of empirical data for exploratory, descriptive, or explanatory purposes. The present review was not limited to experimental studies, as many other reviews of social work effectiveness have been. Research for purposes of exploration and description was considered equally valuable to the development of clinical knowledge. In instances where research reviews already exist, as in the social work effectiveness debate, the present review presents a review of reviews rather than a re-analysis of original findings.

Substantively, studies selected for the present review were limited to investigations of clinical social work. Studies related to child welfare, public welfare, and macro methods were excluded. The organization of the present review and the framework for several chapters were borrowed from the psychotherapy reviews of Garfield and Bergin (Bergin & Garfield, 1971; Garfield & Bergin, 1978, 1986). Just as social work has borrowed from knowledge developed in other fields, clinical research in social work has been heavily influenced by research in psychotherapy. Social work research, however, has not been confined within the parameters of psychotherapy research but has extended beyond them in considering the social context of all participants in the clinical enterprise. The organizational framework for the present review follows.

Components of the Clinical Process

In the clinical process, an individual or small group receives help with a psychosocial problem or concern through the purposive action of a trained clinician. It is a multifaceted and complex transaction that takes place in and is influenced by an even more complex social environment. To investigate and understand this process, a method of subdividing the process into component parts is required so that each component can be examined individually as well as in combination with others.

On a rudimentary level, the clinical process can be perceived as analogous to data processing in that both have input, process, and outcome components. Input, in the clinical context, refers to the raw materials of the clinical process, elements such as client, clinician, and problem that come together for a specific purpose. Process denotes the interaction that ensues between the input components, such as clinician behavior and client response. Process also refers to structures that define the nature of interactions, such as entry and contracting. Outcome refers to the products or results of the interaction; in the clinical context this typically translates into problem reduction and/or goal attainment.

This conceptualization, while elementary, has proved useful for organizing clinical research inasmuch as studies generally focus either on one category of variables or on associations between two categories, such as input and outcome. Psychotherapy reviews, such as Bergin and Garfield's (1986), have been organized according to this framework, and because social work research in many instances has evolved from psychotherapy research, this framework is useful for the present review. Within each of these categories, however, social work research has extended beyond psychotherapy research by encompassing social contexts in addition to psychological factors.

In addition to the three categories of input, process, and outcome, a separate category for training has been added. Training, which refers here to clinician training, can be considered part of input, subsumed under clinician traits specific to therapy, but the present review considers training in a wider context. Training is considered a process itself, parallel to the clinical process in that it involves input components, such as students and professors, process components, such as programs and structures, and outcomes in terms of knowledge and performance. The training process, therefore, warrants a separate and comprehensive review.

The input, process, outcome, and training components of clinical process as they appear in social work research are presented in Figure 1-1. An overview of these elements is provided in this chapter; subsequent chapters discuss specific research in each area.

Input

The elements of the clinical relationship, which come together for a therapeutic or ameliorative purpose, can be thought of as clinical input. Both clinicians and researchers need to understand these components to be able to identify and monitor salient variables and to determine the ways in which these variables relate or interact to produce various outcomes. Input variables typically considered in clinical research include client characteristics, client environments, client problems, clinician attributes, and clinical environments.

Clients. Client variables have been studied to obtain descriptions or profiles of social work clients and to determine the characteristics of individuals considered to be in need of social work services. Demographic characteristics such as age, sex, education, and marital status, have been surveyed. Demographic characteristics have also been studied to investigate how clients differ from nonclients and the associations of client characteristics with other variables. Since social work clients vary considerably by setting, the investigation of client characteristics has been setting-specific with primary foci on family service agencies, mental health clinics, and hospital social service departments. In each instance, findings regarding client characteristics have had implications for delivery of clinical services.

Psychological variables of clients have also been investigated in social work studies. Although intensive or global personality assessments have not

INPUT
Clients
  Demographic characteristics
  Psychological characteristics
  Social characteristics
  Problems
Clinicians
  Extratherapy characteristics
  Therapy-specific traits
Clinical environments
  Stress and burnout
  Supervision

PROCESS
Engagement
  Screening, referral, help-seeking
Adherence
  Client factors
  Treatment factors
Contract negotiations
  Communication
  Parameters of intervention
Components of process

OUTCOME
Individual intervention
Couple and family intervention
Group intervention

TRAINING
Students
Programs
Educators
Methods

Figure 1.1. Components of the Clinical Process.

been considered within the purview of social work, investigations of variables such as locus of control and interpersonal attraction have been studied.

Social factors impinging on clients, such as socio-economic status and availability of social support, have been subjects of clinical research in social work.

An understanding of the nature of the problems that confront clients is necessary to provide appropriate clinical intervention. The range of client problems presented to clinical social workers has been vast and is beyond the scope of the present review. Social workers, however, have developed and utilized a number of problem classification systems, and the research on these systems will be reviewed. Since the problems typically addressed by social workers tend to vary by agency, typologies have tended to be setting-specific. The primary typologies used by social workers were developed for hospital social services, family services, and mental health settings. A few generic social work problem typologies have also been studied. Research regarding client factors, including social contexts and problem typologies, is reviewed in Chapter 2.

Clinicians. An understanding of clinicians in the clinical process is important because clinicians direct process and provide interventions. The manner in which this is done and the effect it has is influenced by various clinician characteristics. Clinician attributes that have been studied can be subdivided into extratherapy and therapy-specific factors. Extratherapy characteristics are not specific to the clinical relationship but rather are general characteristics of clinicians, such as age, sex, ethnicity, socio-economic status, values, and attitudes. Therapy- or intervention-specific characteristics include clinician training, expectations, style, presentation of facilitative conditions, theoretical orientation, and vendorship. Clinician traits typically have been studied singly or in conjunction with client characteristics to determine the effect of clinician attributes on clinical outcomes. A review of studies related to clinician characteristics is presented in Chapter 3.

Clinical environments. Clinical environments have been studied based on the assumption that environments affect clinicians, who in turn affect clients and clinical outcomes. Studies of environments hence have focused primarily on the effect of environmental factors on clinicians, designating clinician job satisfaction and burnout as products of various environmental conditions. Supervision also has been studied in this context because it has been hypothesized to serve as a buffer or mediator of various environmental factors. Studies of clinical environments are reviewed in Chapter 4.

In summary, the input components or raw materials of the clinical process have been investigated to determine their effects, singly or in combination, on clinical processes and outcomes. The clinical process that ensues when input components are combined has also been examined.

Process

Clinical process, the interactive system produced by the coming together of input components, also has been studied. Topics investigated have included initial engagement or entry into the clinical relationship, development of relationship parameters including contracting and adherence to contracts, and communications between clinician and client.

Engagement. Entry and engagement in clinical processes have been studied in terms of both client and clinician factors. Client factors that have been studied include the decision to seek help, the sources of help utilized, and the timing of help-seeking. Clinical factors studied in relation to engagement include the screening and referral processes.

Adherence. Adherence to clinical regimens, including continuance in treatment, has been studied in terms of both client and intervention factors.

Contract negotiation. Contracts between clients and clinicians involve specification of parameters such as the term and duration of interventions. The effects of these parameters on clinical outcome have been studied. The process of negotiation or initial communication between clients and clinicians has also been the subject of social work study.

Components of process. Interactions between clients and clinicians, primarily communication processes, have been analyzed using several specific clinical models. Process analysis of mediating, family therapy, and feminist models of intervention have been reviewed. Research on clinical processes is reviewed in Chapter 5.

Outcome

Clinical practice and clinical research are both activities aimed at promoting positive client outcomes. Clinical interventions involving individual clients, couples, families, and small groups have been evaluated in terms of outcome. Clinical studies have also investigated whether social work intervention provides any demonstrable benefit over no intervention. More specific studies have evaluated the relative benefits of different types of interventions. A review of the social work effectiveness debate, with specific reference to studies of individual interventions, is presented in Chapter 6.

Methodological issues in the investigation of social work interventions are reviewed in Chapter 6, and studies related to effectiveness of group intervention are reviewed in Chapter 7. Since the evaluation of outcome requires definition of intervention methods as well as purposes, the literature regarding definition of social group work is briefly reviewed, along with issues of measurement and analysis of group data.

Studies related to the effectiveness of marital and family interventions are reviewed in Chapter 8. The review of this research was organized according to major problem types presented in the literature.

In summary, outcome studies have been linked with various intervention modalities, including individual, group, and family. Within each of these, efforts have been made to establish the specific characteristics of clinical social work intervention. Comparative studies within modalities, however, have been few.

Training

Studies related to the training of clinical social workers are reviewed in Chapter 9. These studies are organized in terms of input, namely, students, professors, and programs; in terms of process, namely, program delivery; and in terms of outcome using different teaching modalities.

Chapter 2

CHARACTERISTICS OF CLIENTS AND THEIR PROBLEMS

Clients represent the primary and most obvious input variable in the clinical equation. Clients and their problems are the raw materials with which clinicians work, and the raison d'etre for the practice of clinical social work. Given the obvious importance of clients and their problems, it is surprising how little these variables have been investigated in social work research. Clinical social workers frequently operate without good information about the range and variability of client characteristics or client problems within their caseloads, how clients differ from nonclients, or how differences between clients and types of problems call for different interventions to increase likelihood of successful outcome.

This chapter reviews research pertinent to client characteristics and problems by type of social work setting. Clinical social workers operate in a number of settings, such as hospitals, family service agencies, and mental health clinics in which client populations have specific and distinct characteristics and present with quite different problems. Given this diversity, generalizations across settings cannot readily be made. This is in contrast to psychotherapy studies in which specific settings are rarely considered.

Studies of social work clients also differ from studies of psychotherapy clients in the greater attention paid to contextual or environmental factors. Garfield (1986) noted that while psychotherapy studies increasingly recognized the impact of external life events, studies of these factors were rare. Social work studies, in contrast, have attended more to contextual factors, primarily those that have been instrumental in providing social support to clients.

Clinical social workers typically provide generalist or eclectic interventions and make treatment decisions on the basis of clinical experience, theoretical orientation, or intuition. Client variables are not always systematically considered in structuring therapeutic encounters. The importance and relevance of client characteristics in this process, therefore, need to be considered.

CLIENT CHARACTERISTICS

Client characteristics, including demographic, psychological, and social variables, have been found to be important in assessing presenting problems, in assessing the appropriateness, extent, and intensity of clinical interventions, and in making decisions about the focus and type of intervention to be provided. Clinicians unmindful of client variables have been said to be operating on the "client uniformity myth" wherein clients are assumed to be similar and interchangeable (Kiesler, 1971). Adherence to this notion of client uniformity, either wittingly or unwittingly, has resulted in application of clinical interventions that were developed for one population to a different population without consideration of the appropriateness of the application. For example, much of the critique regarding treatment of women in clinical social work has been based on lack of clinician attention to gender-specific characteristics (Burden & Gottlieb, 1987). Interventions developed for one gender have not always transposed successfully to the other. Similarly client characteristics such as age, race, education, and economic status, in some instances, have been found to render particular interventions less than effective.

Understanding the ways in which client populations differ from comparable nonclient populations has also been found to be helpful in deciding on appropriate interventive foci. Understanding that women who are depressed are more likely to also be maritally distressed than women who are not depressed can alert clinicians to intervene in marital as well as individual problems (Weissman, 1980). Similarly the knowledge that differences between assaultive couples and equally conflicted but nonassaultive couples lies primarily in differences among the men has implications for the focus of clinical interventions (Russell, Lipov, Phillips, & White, 1989). Lack of specific knowledge about client and nonclient differences can lead to over-

or underestimation of client problems or pathology, since normative comparisons are not available.

Clinical choices about the duration and intensity of clinical interventions also can be improved through knowledge of the range and variability of client characteristics. Specht and Specht (1986) discussed the importance of assessment of client personal resources in making allocations of expensive and limited clinical interventions. Clinicians who make such decisions regularly can benefit from good data on which to base their expert judgments.

Decisions about the most appropriate type or method of intervention similarly can benefit from a consideration of client characteristics. Not all clients benefit equally from all types of interventions. For example, clients suffering from severe environmental deprivation are unlikely to benefit from psychodynamic interventions until some of their more basic needs have been met. Increased knowledge about both client characteristics and their interaction with clinical interventions is necessary to increase treatment effectiveness.

Even when they are aware of the benefits of a comprehensive client data base, clinical social workers at times have been reluctant to use it. Using client information to make treatment decisions has been viewed as conflicting with social values such as universality of service, the individual's democratic right to treatment, and social justice for the underprivileged. However, as Specht and Specht (1986) have discussed, decisions about service entitlement are different from clinical decisions and should be decided on different levels. Social judgments about service entitlement should be made prior to clinical encounters and should be made by policy makers, not clinicians. Clinical judgments, in contrast, are based on clinical expertise and knowledge about a variety of factors, including client characteristics, and are necessary to ensure that the best service is provided.

Clinicians' reluctance to collect client data regularly and systematically has also been attributed to lack of accord between clinicians' perceptions regarding clinical outcome and the findings of clinical research. It has been suggested that at least one reason for this observed discrepancy may lie in different definitions of what constitutes clienthood. Some discussion of clienthood, therefore, is warranted.

Definition of Clienthood

Research definitions of clienthood have included both cross-sectional definitions, in which every person registered as an active case on a given date was considered a client, and longitudinal definitions, in which every new person registering for or receiving service over a specified period was considered a client. The former definition allows for descriptions of the *prevalence* of variables, whereas the latter allows for descriptions of *incidence* of variables. In either instance, all persons receiving or registered for service were considered clients.

These commonly accepted definitions of clienthood, however, have been criticized for being too broad. It has been suggested that individuals who seek clinical service can be either *applicants* for service, who apply for but subsequently fail to enter into a clinical relationship; *consumers* of service, who apply for and receive concrete or specific services without entering a clinical relationship; and *true clients,* who apply for and enter into a clinical relationship with a professional (Alcabes & Jones, 1985; Specht & Specht, 1986). To be a bona fide client, this argument holds, applicants for service first must be assessed for eligibility, socialized into a client role, and entered into a clinical contract. According to this definition, failure to complete eligibility assessment, socialization, or contracting, through client drop-out or clinician advice, results in failure to achieve clienthood.

These separate categories of applicant, consumer, and client, it has been argued, should be adopted by clinical researchers in order to obtain more valid measures of client outcome. However, researchers have not overwhelmingly adopted this suggestion, probably due to the post hoc nature of the definitions. Using these definitions, it is not possible to determine whether an individual is a true client until service has been completed. The definition of clienthood therefore is dependent on, rather than separate from, outcome.

Determination of clienthood is an important aspect of both practice and research. However, definitions of clienthood need to be based on screening criteria that are well-defined at the outset, not determined on the basis of subsequent clinical outcome. The following discussion of client characteristics is based on a definition of clienthood that does not distinguish between applicants, consumers, and clients, but rather regards as clients all persons seeking and receiving social work services.

Demographic Characteristics

Studies of the demographic characteristics of clinical social work clients have tended to be setting-specific due to the considerable variability of these characteristics across settings. Studies of psychological and social attributes, in contrast, have been generalized across settings. Inasmuch as clinical social workers are largely employed in psychotherapeutic settings (Kutchins & Kirk, 1989) and psychotherapy clients have been the most extensively studied, a summary of psychotherapy findings provides a useful starting point for the present review.

Psychotherapy Clients

Clients receiving psychotherapeutic services typically have been studied as an undifferentiated group. Distinctions have not been drawn between different types of clinical settings or professional affiliations of service providers. Recipients of services provided by psychiatrists, psychologists, and social workers have typically been regarded uniformly as psychotherapy or counseling clientele.

The rationale for studying client characteristics in psychotherapy investigations has been to determine the association of these characteristics with therapy outcomes (Garfield, 1978; Lambert & Asay, 1984). Primarily, attention has been given to the variables of sex, age, marital status, and education.

Sex. In reviewing studies of client sex, Marecek and Johnson (1980) noted that more women typically seek psychotherapy than men. Results of studies of proportional representation in clinical caseloads, however, have been mixed. Several studies have found that equal proportions of each sex were accepted for treatment; others have found that women, especially married women, were most likely to be accepted for treatment. Studies of caseload composition by profession have found that psychiatrists were more likely to prefer female clients and have all female caseloads than psychologists or social workers, whose caseloads tended to be more balanced. Whether this finding reflected the greater selective control that psychiatrists had over their caseloads was not determined.

Several analogous studies involving social workers providing psychotherapeutic services have investigated the effect of client sex. A study of 298 Hawaiian social workers found that they rated female clients higher in intelligence, maturity, and treatment responsiveness than male clients (Fischer, Dulaney, Fazio, Hudak & Zivotofsky, 1976). In a more recent study, social work students also favored female clients, although each sex was rated less mature when rated by a social worker of the same sex (Gingerich & Kirk, 1981). Dailey (1983) suggested that sex may be less important than sex-role identification in client ratings and demonstrated that androgynous clients, or those demonstrating both male and female traits, were judged more favorably by social workers than comparable clients who demonstrated traditional sex-roles. All of these studies, however, involved ratings of client vignettes rather than actual clients in clinical situations, thus raising the question of the extent these findings can be generalized to the real clinical situations.

Reviews of psychotherapy studies have concluded that sex is not a determining factor in outcome, but that in particular situations same-sex pairings may be more conducive to positive outcome (Garfield, 1986; Lambert & Asay, 1984). Furthermore, for treatment of some problems, such as sexual assault, same-sex pairing of client and clinician has been advised.

Age. Psychotherapy clients typically have tended to be in their late 20s or early 30s, with median ages of 27 and 32 reported in one study (Garfield, 1978). Lambert & Asay (1984) suggested that this finding could be a function of selection, as therapists prefer to work with younger clients and may more readily reject clients over 40 than younger ones. In terms of outcome, the results have not consistently supported age as a significant factor in determining outcome. It has, however, been suggested that age-matching of clients and therapists may be conducive to continuation in therapy and positive outcome.

Marital status. As noted previously, evidence suggests that therapists prefer married women as clients, but there are no reports that married clients are overrepresented in client populations. Neither is there substantial evidence that marital status correlates with outcome. One study, however, reported a positive trend when clients and therapists were matched on marital status, confirming the emerging trend that favors client-clinician matching (Lambert & Asay, 1984).

Education. Educational levels of clients are likely to be a function of both social class and intelligence, and all three factors have been studied independently. In each case, a selective factor appears to predominate, with therapists preferring clients of higher social class, educational level, and intelligence. Commenting on one study that reported mean client IQs of 117 and 112, Garfield noted that using such criteria 75% of the population would be rendered ineligible for therapy. However, once a person is accepted into the client pool there appears to be only a modest correlation of intelligence with therapy outcome (Garfield, 1978; Lambert & Asay, 1984). Intelligence and education, however, may be factors that determine the type of treatment provided, with insight-oriented therapists preferring highly verbal, articulate clients, and behaviorally oriented therapists reporting positive outcomes with clients of varying intellectual levels, including mentally retarded clients.

While psychotherapy clients have been studied en masse, social work clients have been studied largely in the context of particular settings. The three primary settings that have been surveyed are family service agencies, mental health settings, and hospital social service departments.

Family Service Clients

Because a large part of the services provided by family-service-type agencies are psychotherapeutic, a considerable overlap in client characteristics can be expected in these two settings. Beck and Jones (1973, 1974) reported a nationwide survey of family service clients that yielded results parallel to the results of psychotherapy client surveys. Family service clients were found to be predominantly in their 20s and 30s and female.

Divorced and separated individuals were overrepresented in the client population, and this proportion was observed to have increased over the past decade. The rate of marital separation in the client population was three times greater than the rate for a comparable age cohort in the general population; the divorce rate was double. Twice as many single-mother families were reported in the client population as in the general population.

Educationally, family service clients typically had completed high school or better, comparable to the general population. However, gains in educational levels in the client population over the past decade failed to match the gains in the general population. This relative decline in the client population was attributed to agencies' outreach programs that had encouraged greater involvement with socially disadvantaged groups.

The association of client characteristics with outcome was also investigated by Beck and Jones (1973). With the exception of age, demographic characteristics were not found to be associated with outcome. A negative correlation between age and outcome was observed, suggesting a "pile-up with age of the problems of daily living, combined with a certain loss of initiative and opportunity for doing something about them" (p. 117). Socioeconomic status was not found to be associated with outcome, suggesting an accommodation to the needs and problems of the disadvantaged by family service agencies. The primary factors associated with outcome were problem severity and degree of client involvement in seeking service.

In summary, family service clients appear to be a somewhat more diverse population than psychotherapy clients, particularly in relation to marital status and socio-economic status. However, evidence to date suggests that family service agencies have accommodated to these differences and tailored their services to meet the needs of their particular clientele.

Mental Health Clinic Clients

In recent years community mental health clinics have included provision of aftercare services to individuals discharged from mental institutions in their mandate. The characteristics of this population and the association of these characteristics with successful community tenure have been the subjects of several social work studies.

Several studies have suggested that the provision of aftercare service itself can predict community tenure. Smith and Smith (1979) in a study of 130 clients found that regular use of aftercare service and a supportive family situation were significantly related to positive adjustment and low recidivism. In contrast, a follow-up of 332 clients by Nuehring and Ladner (1980) found that aftercare attendance increased the likelihood of rehospitalization. They also found that aftercare attendance was correlated with youth, medication usage, a history of prior hospitalizations, and less adequate functioning in social roles. The authors maintained, however, that situational variables, particularly clinic attendance, were more predictive of rehospitalization than symptoms or behaviors. Selig (1980) reached a similar conclusion in a follow-up study of 57 discharged clients, finding that readmission did not result from symptoms, but was associated largely with low income and after-care provided by a clinic, as opposed to a private physician. Aftercare provided by physicians, however, also was more likely to be provided to clients with higher education, more responsible social roles, and more stable marital situations. The evidence regarding aftercare, hence, remains mixed, since individuals utilizing aftercare tend to be more deficient in social and personal resources, and thus more vulnerable to recurrence of distress.

Studies of mental health clinic clients have noted the emergence of a particular subpopulation characterized by youth and marginal social integration. This group has been labeled the "new, young chronics" (Canton, 1981). McCreath (1984) surveyed the intake of a mental health center for an 18-month period and found that the majority of clients (78%) fell into the young adult group. They were primarily male, single, well-educated, and living with parents and were likely to have had their first psychiatric contact before the age of 20. Davis (1986) similarly found a preponderance of single males with early psychiatric contact in the young chronic group, as compared to a more even sex distribution among an older group attending a mental health center. Furthermore, the younger group utilized both hospital and clinic services more often and were more unstable in their living and work situations than the older group. Christ (1984) also found that the group most likely to experience delays in discharge from psychiatric hospital was young, single, and without family support.

A high degree of substance abuse among the young chronic group, which served to further exacerbate their problems, has been documented in several studies (Solomon & Davis, 1986; Walsh, 1986). The conclusion reached by most studies of the young chronic population has been that these clients present a novel and complex challenge to established treatment methods.

Hospital Social Service Clients

In the past client caseloads of hospital social workers were largely a function of the referral process because medical personnel initiated requests for client contact. The results of this referral system, as compared to social work casefinding, has been the subject of several studies by Berkman (nee Gordon) and Rehr (Berkman & Rehr, 1970, 1973; Gordon & Rehr, 1969). These studies found that the clients referred by medical personnel were largely elderly persons over 75, primarily women, unmarried, and disproportionately nonwhite. With social work casefinding, the proportion of white clients and women increased. More importantly, however, social workers identified clients earlier in their hospital stay and thereby increased the likelihood of early discharge (Boone, Coulton, & Keller, 1982).

Social work identification of high-risk clients has led to the development of early screening procedures (Rehr, Berkman, & Rosenberg, 1980). A number of studies have attempted to evaluate these screening procedures, but the results have been inconclusive. Methodological difficulties, such as lack of sensitivity or overinclusiveness of screening mechanisms and the inadequacy or incompleteness of admission records on which screening is based, have been problems that have limited these studies to date (Becker & Becker, 1986; Berkman, Bedell, Parker, McCarthy, & Rosenbaum, 1988; Berkman, Dumas, Gastfriend, Poplawski, & Southworthe, 1987; Coulton, 1988; Reardon, Blumenfield, Weissman, & Rosenberg, 1988).

The relevance of client characteristics in referrals to social work has been recognized by allied helping professionals. A study of interdisciplinary referral by Dove, Schneider, and Gitelson (1985) found that level of mobility, mental health status, and length of hospital stay were used across disciplines to determine the appropriateness of social work referrals. Similarly, clients' marital status was found to be significantly associated with referral to social workers in an acute psychiatric hospital (Selig, 1978). These studies have underscored the importance of client characteristics in referrals to social work, as well as the importance of social work involvement in the casefinding process.

While the demographic characteristics of clients have been investigated within specific settings, consideration of the psychological characteristics of clients has been more general, based on the assumption that these characteristics generalize across particular types of services.

Psychological Characteristics

Motivation and Expectations

While clinical practitioners recognize that clients vary considerably in their motivation for and expectations of treatment, the clinical investigation of these variables has been fraught with problems of definition and measurement (Garfield, 1986). A commonly accepted definition of motivation has been that of a desire for change congruent with clinician goals and values. It has further been understood as a fluid condition that is subject to change throughout the course of intervention. While several psychotherapy studies have reported correlation between initial motivation and successful outcome, other studies have found initially unmotivated clients to do equally well. It has been suggested that clients may become motivated through clinicians' actions during intervention and that the critical variable is the development of motivation rather than initial client motivation per se.

Investigations of client expectations in psychotherapy studies have tended to show positive correlations with outcome, but critics have suggested that these findings may be spurious, given the self-reported level of both expectations and outcome (Garfield, 1986). Furthermore, considerable divergence exists between studies regarding the definition of expectations, which has varied from expectation of positive outcome, to expectation of therapist proficiency, to expectations regarding the procedures and process of therapy.

Client expectations studied in social work research typically have revealed considerable divergence between client and worker expectations. Mayer and Timms' (1969) British study of clients seeking help for family problems revealed, for example, that clients expected clinicians to make judgments regarding the rightness or wrongness of disputant behaviors as well as to take some ameliorative or coercive action. The clinicians, in contrast, provided insight and psychodynamic explanations of behaviors, which led to considerable client dissatisfaction. Rubenstein and Block (1978), in comparing expectations of clinicians and low-income unmarried mothers in a county welfare office, found considerable agreement in ranking client problems but less agreement in rating the importance of problems. Clinicians tend to place more emphasis on interpersonal relations while clients emphasized resources and training. Despite these differences, clients regarded their clinicians as helpful. Maluccio (1979) found that family service clients tended to expect assistance in crisis resolution, whereas clinicians expected to provide treatment for long-standing psychopathology.

Rosen and Cohen (1980) investigated discrepancies between client expectations and preferences, defining the former as what clients expected to happen and the latter what they would like to happen. Discrepancies between expectations and preferences were found to correlate with continuance in treatment. Furthermore, clients who had a number of preferences that they did not expect to be confirmed perceived themselves as powerless to change the situation but, nevertheless, continued in treatment. Rosen and Cohen suggested that clients who continued in treatment did so because of a sense of inertia or a high dependence on the clinical relationship. Although the results of this study were only suggestive because the correlations obtained were relatively low, the study was unique in combining measures of expectations and preferences with clients' sense of control of the counseling situation.

Increased attention to client expectations in both clinical practice and research in social work is warranted. No social work studies have addressed effect of clinician behaviors on client expectations during intervention. This is a particularly important area of investigation because experimental manipulation of psychotherapy expectations has suggested that these expectations are influenced by clinicians and that they are related to outcome (Garfield, 1986).

Locus of Control

Locus of control has been defined as the extent to which individuals believe in their capacity to control the reinforcing contingencies of their environment. *External control* has been defined as a perception of powerlessness; an inability to control events that occur by luck, chance, fate, or the actions of powerful others. *Internal control*, in contrast, has been defined as the perception that events are contingent on an individual's behavior or on her or his relatively permanent characteristics (Rotter, 1966). This concept has been useful in clinical evaluations; locus of control has been demonstrated to be correlated with psychological adjustment as well as psychotherapy outcome (Phares, 1976). In addition, psychotherapy studies have indicated that the effectiveness of therapeutic modalities may vary with locus of control. Directive approaches, for example, were found to be more beneficial for externally oriented individuals, while nondirective approaches were more beneficial for internally oriented individuals (Abramowitz, Abramowitz, Roback, & Jackson, 1974).

Locus of control of both social workers and their clients was investigated by Latting and Zundel (1986) in their study of differences in world view. This study sought to determine the association of perception of control with perception of blame or responsibility among both clinicians and clients. It was hypothesized that clinicians not only would be more likely to have an internal locus of control and also would be more likely to have an internal or individual, as opposed to social or political, sense of responsibility for problems. The results for clinicians indicated, however, that, while locus of control was internal, locus of responsibility was external. Clients, on the other hand, subscribed to an external locus of control and an internal locus of responsibility. Furthermore, client views were influenced by race and income; minority clients of low income were most likely to endorse the position of individual helplessness combined with individual responsibility or blame for problems.

Goodban (1985) studied client explanations for being on welfare among 100 black single mothers and found that variability in control attribution was related to ideology and class identification. Although the majority of women (60%) espoused an ideology of equal opportunity and individuation, those who endorsed it most strongly held themselves responsible for their poverty status and tended to identify with middle-class status and values. In contrast, those who believed in unequal opportunity for the poor were less likely to blame themselves and identified causal factors within social, situational, or other person realms.

Social work studies of client locus of control thus have raised questions about the validity and relevance of conclusions based on psychotherapy studies of locus of control. Social work clients, who are frequently poor and disadvantaged, appear to ascribe their condition largely to internal factors. The extent to which this facilitates or deters change in client self-perceptions or situations has not been determined. However, because much of social work intervention involves identifying and rectifying external barriers to change, it would seem that a corresponding shift in client perception from internal to external responsibility could be viewed as positive. When social rather than psychological disadvantages or deficits present problems, externalizing both locus of control and responsibility may be desirable. These relationships, however, await further study.

Interpersonal Attraction

Client characteristics that clinicians find attractive have been posited to influence the clinical relationship because clinicians tend to be more involved in relationships with clients they find pleasing. Schofield (1964), for example, coined the YAVIS syndrome on the basis of findings that social workers, psychologists, and psychiatrists all preferred clients who were *Y*outhful, *A*ttractive, *V*erbal, *I*ntelligent, and *S*uccessful. Studies of attractiveness have focused largely on physical attractiveness and verbal expressiveness. Psychotherapy studies have provided substantial evidence that client attractiveness is related to clinical outcome (Garfield, 1986). However, because clinicians provided both ratings of attractiveness and outcome in these studies, contamination of these results is likely.

Social workers, in a Hawaiian study (Cousins, Fischer, Glisson & Kameoka, 1986), were asked to rate clients on both physical attractiveness and verbal expressiveness. Physical attractiveness was not associated with clinician ratings of clients. However, verbal expressiveness was associated with ratings of client trust, adjustment, motivation, and maturity.

In summary, client expectations, locus of control, and interpersonal attractiveness are all factors that have the potential to influence the clinical relationship. Social workers have not been particularly adept in assessing or meeting client expectations, nor have their views on locus of control and responsibility matched those of their clients. Both social work researchers and clinicians need to consider further the effects of these consistently demonstrated discrepancies on clinical outcome.

Social Characteristics

Clinical social work is differentiated from other helping professions in the attention it pays to environmental as well as psychological factors in the clinical process. Clinical research in social work likewise has attended to environmental factors, focusing primarily on socio-economic status and social support as both prognostic indicators and targets for intervention.

Socio-Economic Status (SES)

Psychotherapy reviews have noted that client SES has been associated with both acceptance into treatment and type of treatment received (Garfield, 1978). Higher SES clients were disproportionately represented in outpatient, insight-oriented therapies, whereas lower SES clients were over-represented in inpatient, behavioral modes of treatment. Social work clients are, by agency definition and mandate, frequently of lower SES strata. Even so, social workers' attitudes twoard clients have been shown to vary by client SES.

Three studies have examined the effects of social class on judgments of clinical social workers. Fischer and Miller (1973) found that 360 California social workers viewed lower-class clients significantly more negatively in terms of level of disturbance, prognosis for treatment, and general likability than middle-class clients. Client race also was found to affect clinician ratings, with black clients judged more positively than white clients and low SES white clients judged most harshly of all. A subsequent replication of this study by Franklin (1985), which examined clinician variables as well as client variables, confirmed the earlier findings of a negative prognosis for low SES clients and positive attitudes toward black clients. Clinician experience also was found to be a significant factor; experienced clinicians were more likely to rate lower-class clients as undesirable than inexperienced clinicians. In a subsequent analysis of the data by clinicians' theoretical orientations, Franklin (1986) reported that psychodynamic interventions were preferred for middle-class clients, whereas environmental modification and enhanced social adjustment were prescribed for low SES clients.

Lower SES clients also have been viewed less positively than middle-class clients by student social workers (Briar, 1961; Friedman & Berg, 1978). This judgment, however, was found to vary by student SES in that low SES students tended to assign low SES clients better prognoses than middle-class clients, whereas middle-class students similarly assigned better prognoses to clients of similar SES status (Friedman & Berg, 1978).

In summary, client social class appears to have a significant effect on clinical judgments made by clinicians. Furthermore, this effect has been shown to vary with race, SES, and experience of clinicians. However, because all of these studies were based on ratings of case analogues, there is no direct evidence that actual clinical behavior or clinical outcome is affected. Further study of these factors is therefore warranted.

Social support

The notion that social support can protect clients from or buffer the effects of stress has been widely accepted by clinicians, and corresponding interventions to mobilize support have been developed. Clinical research focused on testing various social support hypotheses has resulted in clarification and specification of earlier statements of the benefits of social support, which were overly general and optimistic.

Definitions of social support initially consisted of measures of concrete provision of aid, affect, or affirmation. The objective delineation of support provided to individuals was referred to as their *social network*. More recently, definitions of social support have emphasized *perceived support,* a subjective evaluation that significant others are caring, available in times of need, and instrumental in providing a satisfying relationship, which is experienced as esteem enhancing or stress reducing (Heller, Swindle, & Dusenbury, 1986). This change in emphasis is the result of cumulative research, which found weak associations between client well-being and various objective measures of network size, density, and so forth, but more sizable associations with measures of subjective appraisal. Furthermore, the results of more than a decade of study of this topic suggest that both the source of support and the types of stress alleviated by support are quite specific and are not readily generalizable (Liberman, 1986). A number of studies, such as the population survey by Denoff (1982), have demonstrated the centrality of spousal support. It has been suggested that support may show a threshold effect in that the critical distinction may lie between having no supportive relationships and having at least one. Also, increasingly the suggestion is made that lack of social support may be correlated with other social and psychological deficiencies (Coyne & DeLongis, 1986).

Several authors have cautioned against uncritical adoption of social support hypotheses without consideration of individual, social, and cultural client factors (Hoch & Hemmans, 1987; Schilling, 1987). Others have suggested the need for careful scrutiny of client needs, resources, and deficits in social network interventions (Auslander & Litwin, 1987; McIntyre, 1986; Specht, 1986). In general, more recent social work reviews have been considerably more critical and more cautious about the type of social support required and the nature and effectiveness of social support interventions than earlier reviews, such as the one by Ell (1984).

A considerable body of social support research in social work has been population specific, focusing on populations of the elderly, women, or individuals with specific health problems. Provision of social support to the elderly, particularly during illness, has been the subject of several studies. In a study of black, urban elderly, Petchers and Milligan (1987) found that family networks were perceived to be available for support during illness. Similarly, Goldberg, Kantrow, Kremen, and Lauter (1986), who studied supports among spouseless, childless elderly women, found that relatives, usually sisters, provided support during illness. Lindenberg and Coulton (1980) also found that family members were the primary support providers following hospital discharge. Stoller (1982) found that a majority of the elderly named a spouse or daughter as a source of assistance in hypothetical illness situations. Gallo (1982, 1984) found that social networks of the elderly were comprised primarily of family members and observed a modest correlation between network size and health status.

In a more detailed analysis, Ell and Haywood (1985) studied recovery from myocardial infarction and found that, while social support was associated with self-esteem, life satisfaction, and personal well-being, it was not associated with health or cardiac status. Furthermore, subjective evaluation of support, rather than the more objective measures of marital status or numbers of household members, was the significant variable. Dhooper (1984) studying a similar population found that social support was correlated with adjustment to illness and also with social class of the patient.

It has been suggested that social support is more important to well-being for women than for men, and several studies have focused on female populations. A correlation between the absence of social support, particularly that provided by a spouse or close companion, and depression in women has been found in a number of studies (Brown, 1987; Camasso & Camasso, 1986). Similarly alcoholic women have reported low levels of support, particularly from an intimate male partner (Schilit & Gomberg, 1987).

Social networks of the severely mentally ill have also been studied and found to be relatively small but not associated with activity level or perceived stress or frustration (Crotty & Kulys, 1985). A study of networks of street drug abusers found their networks to be stable and not affected through residential treatment (Fraser & Hawkins, 1984).

The results of social work studies have largely confirmed the results of earlier psychological studies. Objective measures of social networks have not been as predictive of well-being as subjective perceptions of helpfulness. Intimate relationships have tended to be central sources of support, with family support perceived as available and satisfactory by most elderly respondents but not by emotionally distressed respondents. Positive associations between perceived support and various indices of well-being have been reported, but the mechanism that explains this association has not been determined. Whether support deficiencies cause, are the result of, or simply indicate other personal deficiencies has not been established and requires further study.

CLIENT PROBLEMS

Client problems, like client characteristics and client environments, are a critical input element in the clinical process. Variability in client problems is virtually infinite and beyond the scope of the present discussion. However, social workers in several settings have found themselves working with particular types of problems and have utilized typologies or classification systems to describe the range of problems presented more systematically. These typologies have proved useful for communicating more clearly with clients, as well as other professionals and community members, the nature of the problems that are amenable to social work intervention. Problem typologies have also been useful for identifying particular treatment needs and resources as well as examining variation in treatment duration and outcome. Social workers have used problem typologies developed by other disciplines as well as developed intrinsic classification systems, and both types have been subject to social work inquiry. Problem classifications used in hospitals, mental health clinics, and family service agencies have been studied.

Hospital Settings

Diagnostic Related Groups Classification

Social workers in U.S. hospitals are increasingly affected by a medical classification system, the Diagnostic Related Groups (DRG). This system, based on medical diagnosis, prescribed treatment, and several patient variables has served to formulate and standardize the cost of hospital patient care, by making payment for care prospective rather than retrospective. Caputi and Heiss (1984) described the development of this system in which costs are predetermined on the basis of the 467-category classification system. Reamer (1985) discussed the potential implications of this system for social workers, including a greater emphasis on discharge planning and disincentives for hospitals to admit socially disadvantaged clients in the interests of cost containment. Several social work studies have examined both the anticipated and actual effects of the DRG system as perceived by hospital social workers.

Patchner and Wattenberg (1985) surveyed 19 hospital social service department directors to determine their attitudes toward DRGs, what changes they expected would occur using DRGs, and the plans they were implementing. Directors reported more positive than negative expectations, including increased prestige and greater involvement of social workers with other health team members, increased cooperation between disciplines leading to greater efficiency in patient care, and improved relations with community agencies. Negative expectations reported included the provision of increased services with fewer resources and decreased ability for social workers to provide patient counseling and follow-up.

To determine the extent to which these expectations were realized, a survey of the four-year experience of New Jersey hospital social work directors in using DRGs was completed (Dinnerman, Seaton, & Schlesinger, 1987). A number of earlier predictions were confirmed. A majority of respondents indicated increased interdisciplinary perceptions of social work expertise and influence. Increased demand for social service, as indicated by increased caseload size, was reported; but the increase was compensated for by increased staff in only half of the reporting hospitals. Increased staff time devoted to discharge planning and high-risk screening was reported by a majority of respondents. No consistent changes in community relations or in the provision of family counseling services were reported.

Berkman-Rehr Classification.

The advent of DRGs combined with comprehensive information systems in hospitals has increased the need for a social work problem classification system (Coulton, 1984). Barbara Berkman and Helen Rehr were instrumental in developing such a classification system, which has proved useful not only in describing psychosocial problems amenable to social work intervention, but also in evaluating outcome. The Berkman-Rehr Classification lists 29 problems, including both concrete services, such as home help and transportation, and psychological help, such as coping with hospitalization or interpersonal relationships (Berkman, 1980). In addition, this system allows evaluation of outcome in terms of both problem resolution (rated on a 4-point scale) and referral outcome (a 6-category rating).

To determine the interrater reliability of the system, client ratings were compared with social worker ratings. A study of 343 discharged clients found that clients agreed with social workers' problem perceptions 77% of the time. Disagreements arose primarily because clients perceived receiving social work assistance on a greater number of problems than reported by social workers. Agreement on problem outcome was considerably lower, with complete agreement on only 57% of cases. However, disagreements arose primarily because social workers assigned lower improvement ratings to client problems than clients did. When improvement categories were reduced to simple ratings of *improved* versus *not improved*, the agreement between clients and social workers increased to 86%. Subsequent studies have revealed even higher levels of agreement (Berkman & Rehr, 1978). Efforts to develop measures to rate psychosocial problem severity have also been reported, but acceptable levels of interrater reliability have not been consistently attained (Hedblom, 1988).

The development of a psychosocial problem classification in hospital settings represents a major achievement in clinical social work practice. The development of the system was the result of an extensive series of social work research projects in hospital settings. Similar efforts to determine the ranges of problems presented to social workers in other settings could be expected to produce similar accomplishments.

Mental Health Clinics

Mental health clinicians in North America rely almost exclusively on the problem classification developed by the American Psychiatric Association (APA), the Diagnostic and Statistical Manual of Mental Disorders, presently in its third edition, revised (DSM-IIIR), with the fourth revision scheduled for 1992 (APA, 1987). The merits and limitations of this system with its numerous revisions and the utility of the system for social work have been discussed by Kutchins and Kirk (1986, 1989). As these authors point out, the early claims that DSM-III was a scientific and unbiased system have not been borne out in subsequent investigations, which instead have demonstrated that misapplication of the system is frequently deliberately unscientific.

Social workers' attitudes toward DSM-III were investigated in a survey of NASW members by Kutchins and Kirk (1989). Specifically, attitudes about the unbiased treatment of women, a highly controversial issue sparked by proposed DSM-III revisions, were studied. Respondents were equally divided between social workers who considered the system unfair to women and those who were unsure or thought it was fair. In a separate report of the same survey, Kirk et al. (1989) reported a high level of clinician skepticism about DSM-III; 55% of respondents reported that the system failed to accurately reflect client problems. In addition, considerable evidence of deliberate misuse of DSM diagnoses was found, with 87% of respondents aware of underdiagnosing, or assigning less serious diagnoses than warranted, and 72% aware of overdiagnosing, or assigning a more serious diagnosis than warranted. The former practice was justified on the basis of reducing stigma of mental dysfunction, while the latter was considered necessary to qualify for reimbursement of professional services. Kutchins and Kirk (1987) indicated that such deliberate misdiagnosing leaves social workers open to malpractice litigation.

Despite the dissatisfaction of clinical social workers with the DSM system, there have been few efforts to replace it with a system that more comprehensively represents the psychosocial problems with which social workers deal. Kirk, Siporin, and Kutchins (1989) described work on a Person in Environment (PIE) system, but commented negatively on the system's complexity and heavy reliance on medical diagnoses. Furthermore, the system's lack of an empirically derived base for classifying client problems was perceived as a major weakness. The development of an empirical data base of client problems in mental health settings is necessary before an adequate and comprehensive problem classification system can be developed. The need for expedient action in this regard was emphasized by Hopps (1987), who suggested that utilization of the DSM-III by social workers could be construed as inadvertent remedicalization of mental health care, moving it away from a multidisciplinary base and away from a concern with the social problems of the disadvantaged. A social work problem classification system could focus on the wider spectrum of environmental as well as intrapsychic problems.

Family Service Settings

Typologies developed for family problems have ranged from simple to elaborate. An elaborate system was described by Seaberg (1970), who developed a set of 146 diagnostic categories for describing adolescent dysfunctioning. The system, which was derived from four different social deviance theories, included a wide range of problems, including low self-esteem, educational problems, disregard of limits, and hostile peer relationships. Low interrater reliability, however, was reported by users of this system, who found that distinctions between the numerous categories were difficult to make.

More global systems of problem categories have been used in several large-scale surveys of family service agencies (Beck & Jones, 1973). These surveys were useful in providing data regarding the distributions of types of problems presented by clients. In addition, a 10-year replication of a nationwide study provided data on trends and changes in presenting problems. The problem classification consisted of six categories: marital, parent-child, personal adjustment, family functioning, external world, and other problems. Family service surveys found that marital problems were most frequently presented, followed closely by problems related to children. Although this pattern remained stable over the decade of the repeated surveys, a change was observed within the children's problem category. Problems with adolescents increased. For clinical practitioners in family service agencies, the denotation of such shifts clearly indicates the need to develop increased knowledge and skill in working with adolescent problems.

The degree of correspondence between clients and clinicians in using the family services classification system was investigated by Sirles (1982). High levels of agreement were reported both in classification of problems and in assessment of outcome. Disagreements in classification arose most frequently in the parent-child category, in which clients perceived both a greater incidence of problems and greater improvement than did clinicians. In general, however, client and clinicians were in agreement regarding the types of problems addressed.

General Problem Categories

Reid and Epstein (1972) developed a problem classification system in their research on the task-centered model of practice. This system consisted of eight categories: interpersonal conflict, dissatisfaction in social relations, problems with formal organizations, difficulty in role performance, decision problems, reactive emotional distress, inadequate resources, and other. This system was reported to have high interjudge agreement rates, generally in excess of 85%, and was found to be useful in classifying problems of school children and psychiatric outpatients.

Another classification system that has generated several social work studies was proposed by Mutschler and Rosen (1979), who divided client problems into categories of personal, interpersonal, and environmental. Mutschler and Rosen studied client-clinician agreement on problem ratings and found significant agreement on environmental problems. Ratings of the two other categories revealed significant differences. Clinicians tended to define most problems as personal, whereas clients tended to rate most problems as interpersonal. Clinician ratings of client improvement also tended to be consistently lower than client ratings. In contrast, the interrater agreement between clinicians was reported to be high (Orme & Gillespie, 1986).

Proctor and Rosen (1983) studied the effects of the Mutschler and Rosen system on treatment planning and found that the number of problems, number of outcomes, and links between problems and outcome were associated with problem category. Clinicians who perceived problems as personal identified a greater number of problems, formulated fewer outcomes or goals, and were more likely to link problems with outcome than clinicians who perceived problems as situational.

Social work researchers' proclivity for using the personal category of problem classification was investigated by Kagle and Cowger (1984). They surveyed practice research published between 1973 and 1982, and found 26 studies, 20 of which defined client problems and measured outcomes in person-centered terms. In 23 of the studies, the environment was neither perceived as part of the problem nor as part of the solution. The authors speculated that this focus partly reflected research conventions as well as availability of technology, inasmuch as both areas were better developed for personal than environmental factors.

SUMMARY

The lack of adequate problem classification systems in most social work settings places clinical social workers at a decided disadvantage. In some settings, such as mental health settings, a problem classification system developed by another discipline has become the operative system. Considerable dissatisfaction among social workers has accrued, but alternate systems have not been developed. In other instances, social work systems have been developed, but because of their highly general nature, they lack the specificity necessary for adequate communication and evaluation of social work functions.

The best example of a social work problem classification system developed to date has been in hospital settings. This system has the merit of being developed on an empirical data base as well as having demonstrated high levels of reliability and validity. Further development along these lines in other social work settings would be of benefit.

Chapter 3

CHARACTERISTICS OF CLINICIANS

Clinicians bring themselves—their personal attributes and their clinical skills and expertise—to the clinical encounter. Clinicians engage with clients in the expectation that their attributes and behaviors will help clients to reach their clinical goals. The extent to which clinician attributes promote or hinder such goal attainment has been the subject of clinical inquiry.

IMPORTANCE OF CLINICIAN ATTRIBUTES

The study of clinician attributes is important in determining how clinician factors affect both clinical processes and clinical outcomes. In spite of this, clinician attributes have received considerably less theoretical and empirical attention than corresponding client attributes. To some extent, this may reflect a reluctance on the part of clinicians to examine themselves, their attitudes and behaviors in the clinical process. Certainly the study of clinician attributes has the potential to disenfranchise entire subpopulations of clinicians from specific interventions if immutable clinician traits are found to predict negative outcomes. Therefore, the study of clinician attributes is not likely to be greeted by clinicians with a great deal of enthusiasm, and their reluctance to pursue this area of investigation can be understood. However, equal investigation of all input variables in the clinical process is warranted until such time as the preeminence of any one variable is determined.

Clinician attributes have been more widely and more extensively investigated in the psychotherapy literature than in the social work literature. Studies of social worker attributes have focused largely on clinician attitudes and theoretical orientations. Typically these studies have been surveys that attempted to aggregate data about social workers in general, rather than to establish the impact of attitudes or other attributes on clinical outcomes. The goal of psychotherapy studies, in contrast, has been to investigate the effects of clinician variables on outcomes; a few social work studies have replicated such studies with social work populations.

The present review includes results of studies of therapist variables in psychotherapy as background to social work research. The division of therapist variables into extratherapy and therapy-specific categories in psychotherapy research has been adopted for the present review, as this distinction pertains as much to clinical social work as to psychotherapy. Both the psychotherapy review and its organization are based largely on the work of Beutler, Crago, and Arizmendi (1986).

EXTRATHERAPY CHARACTERISTICS

Extratherapy characteristics, or characteristics that therapists unwittingly or irrelevantly bring to the therapeutic process, include both externally served characteristics, or sociodemographic traits such as age, sex, race, and socio-economic status, and inferred internal characteristics such as personality traits and expectations.

Past reviews of clinician variables have focused on the effects of these variables independent of client characteristics; more recently the trend has been to study clinician-client matching. The results of matching studies have tended to support, albeit weakly, the benefits of client-clinician matching under specific conditions. The incremental gains derived through matching have been relatively small and primarily have affected engagement in, rather than outcome of, the clinical process (Beutler, Crago, & Arizmendi, 1986). The results of investigations of several different variables will be presented in turn.

Age

Isolating the effect of age in clinical interventions has proved difficult because age is typically associated with experience. Furthermore, the direction of the age difference can be relevant. Clinicians who are older than clients are likely to be perceived quite differently than clinicians who are younger. Donnan and Mitchell's (1979) findings supported the hypothesis that clinicians who were older than their clients were more positively perceived than clinicians who were younger than their clients. Younger clinicians were perceived by older clients as insufficiently wise and too immature. Problem type also appeared to have some bearing on the age of clinicians preferred by clients. For example, adolescents with personal problems preferred clinicians of similar age, whereas adolescents with career problems preferred older clinicians (Getz & Miles, 1978). In general, psychotherapy studies have found that age similarity tended to have a modest effect on therapeutic outcome. The direction of age difference and the nature of client problem both influenced client preferences regarding clinician age.

Beck's (1987) survey of family service clinicians supported the importance of directionality of age differences and type of problem. Outcome of family relations problems, particularly those involving children, was significantly affected by age matching. Specifically, clients under 55 achieved less positive outcomes with clinicians 10 or more years younger than themselves, but this was not true of clients over 55. In fact, clients over 55 did somewhat better with younger clinicians, although this trend did not reach a level of statistical significance. With other problem types, age matching was not a significant factor.

Sex

In psychotherapy studies, same sex client-clinician dyads have fairly consistently been rated by clients as superior to mixed sex dyads with the exception of a few studies in which female clinicians were favored by both male and female clients (Beutler et al., 1986). However, clinician gender may be less important than clinician attitudes about sex roles. Clinicians who conveyed liberalism, flexibility, and egalitarianism in sex roles were more positively rated, regardless of their sex per se.

Social work studies of clinician sex have primarily investigated the effect of sex on clinical judgments using case vignettes or clinical analogues. In a survey of 289 Hawaiian social workers, both male and female clinicians responded more favorably to clients of their own sex (Fischer, Dulaney, Fazio, Hudak, & Zivotofsky, 1976). Dailey (1980) replicated this study with 207 Kansas social workers but failed to find any benefits of sex matching. To further investigate whether sex-role attitudes rather than clinician sex was a significant factor, Dailey (1983) compared the judgments of clinicians typed as masculine, feminine, and androgynous. However, only one of 11 clinical judgments was affected by clinician sex-typing and that favored androgynous over feminine clinicians.

Jayaratne and Ivey (1981) asked social workers to provide descriptions of their most recent client and analyzed them according to sex of clinician and client. Male clinicians did not vary in their descriptions by client sex, but female clinicians tended to be more negative toward female than male clients.

In an attempt to improve on the paper-and-pencil methodology of the previous studies, Gingerich and Kirk (1981) used videotaped client presentations. Only ratings of eye contact and self-depreciation, however, were more positive for same sex pairs.

In contrast to analogue studies, Beck (1987b) studied actual client-clinician dyads in family service agencies. No support was found for sex matching. Instead, results indicated the superiority of female clinicians with both male and female clients. Drop-out rates were also lower for female clinicians.

Combined effects of clinician sex and profession were investigated by Alperin and Neidengard (1984) in a survey of 120 male inpatients of an alcohol detoxification center. Although sex was not found to be relevant in client ratings of psychologist or psychiatrist expertness, female social workers were rated as less expert than male social workers. All social workers, however, were rated as having less influence than members of the other two professions.

Clinician sex has been found to correlate with general measures of attitudes toward women and general attributions of control and responsibility. Two studies found that female social workers had more liberal attitudes toward women than male social workers (Brown & Hellinger, 1975; Davenport & Reims, 1978). Opposite findings were reported in a survey of public assistance workers by Day (1979), who reported that female clinicians, particularly in small counties, had stereotypic views of women. However, no statistical analyses of data were reported.

Attributions of control over individual success and failure have been found to vary by sex among social workers, with female social workers significantly more likely to attribute control to environmental, or uncontrollable, forces than male social workers (Jayaratne & Ivey, 1981). Clinical social workers as a group were found to have a more external orientation than a comparative general population group, a finding that was considered surprising given the presumed internal focus of clinical interventions.

Social worker status has also been found to vary with sex. Higher salaries and higher job responsibilities have been reported for male than for female social workers (Fanshel, 1976; Jennings & Dailey, 1979; Knapman, 1977; Williams, Ho, & Fielder, 1974). Subsequent investigations that studied the interaction of experience, rank, and salary again demonstrated that male clinicians were not only more likely to rise to higher positions than female clinicians but also to receive greater salary increments as they did so (Yamatani, 1982). Among social work educators, Gould and Kim (1976) found significantly higher salaries among males even when rank, doctorate, publication, experience, and ethnicity were controlled. In a replication of this study, Rubin (1981) confirmed the statistical difference between male and female salaries, but suggested that the magnitude was "miniscule," and in a subsequent analysis of rank by sex that confirmed the preponderance of male faculty in senior ranks, suggested that the magnitude of the association was negligible (Rubin, 1982). It is unlikely that lesser paid female faculty relegated to junior ranks would concur with these conclusions.

Ethnicity

Ethnic client-clinician matching has been found in most psychotherapy studies to benefit the therapeutic process (Beutler et al., 1986), particularly in the early engagement phase, where dropping out appears to be decreased by ethnic matching. The observed benefits of matching, however, tend to be less evident at termination or follow-up. It has been suggested, however, that lack of ethnic matching, even when it does not result in client drop-out, can have subtle effects on clinical processes, such as overestimation of pathology, underestimation of prognosis, and treatment streaming. These subtle differences may influence the clinical process but not be discovered through traditional outcome evaluation. It has been further suggested that ethnic diversity itself may not be the operative factor, but rather clinician attitudes toward ethnically divergent groups may be the salient variable that affects the clinical relationship.

In a study of social workers, Turner (1970) investigated differences between French- and English-speaking clients and clinicians in central Canada, finding differences in outcome by client ethnicity and differences in clinician behavior by ethnicity. However, results of client-clinician matching were not reported. Chandler (1980) surveyed 68 social workers to determine their self-perceived competency in cross-cultural counseling and found that the majority of respondents felt most competent with clients of their own ethnic group. Beck (1987b), studying family service clients and clinicians, found consistent evidence for improved outcome when client-clinician dyads were matched for ethnicity.

Socio-Economic Status

The effect of clinician socio-economic status (SES) on therapeutic process and outcome has been a relatively unexplored area in psychotherapy and social work. Factors mitigating against study of clinician SES include the frequently made assumption that clinicians present a relatively homogeneous socio-economic group, controversy about whether present SES or SES of family of origin should be assessed, observations that clinicians are unreliable in reporting client SES and biased in overestimating SES similarity with their clients, and uncertainty about the mechanism by which clinician SES impacts therapy. Again, it has been suggested that it may be clinician egalitarianism toward low SES clients, rather than status per se, that influences the clinical process. Psychotherapy studies have provided some evidence that SES matching has clinical benefits, but this is more likely due to the superior prognosis of high SES clients, who are also most likely to match clinicians' SES status (Beutler et al., 1986).

Beck (1987b) studied family service clients and clinicians to determine the effects of matching by SES factors and found that distance rather than proximity was associated with positive outcome. Clinicians of higher SES origins achieved their highest client outcome ratings from the lowest status clients and their worst ratings from upper status clients. For clinicians of lower SES origins, the opposite pattern prevailed. This trend was particularly strong for clients with family relationship problems. Beck similarly found that disparity rather than commonality was beneficial with regard to marital status and parenthood. Single clinicians without children had the best outcome ratings with clients presenting with family relationship problems.

Attitudes and Values

The myths of value-free clinicians and value-free clinical processes have repeatedly been shattered by empirical research in psychotherapy. When clinician and client attitudes have been monitored, the results have consistently indicated that successful psychotherapy is characterized by initial attitude divergence followed by convergence, primarily due to client adoption of clinician attitudes. Whether this convergence causes improvement, or simply provides an index of improvement, however, has not been established (Beutler, 1981). Furthermore, therapeutic improvement appears, to some extent, to be a function of the clinician's ability to be accepting or tolerant of the client's attitudes, whereas clients respond more positively to clinician rejection of some of their beliefs. It appears that a perception of movement in therapy has been associated with the influence of clinicians in changing attitudes or perceptions of their clients.

The majority of attitudinal studies of social workers have been specific to particular client populations and are discussed in the therapy-specific section. Other studies of values and attitudes, which have been conducted primarily on social work students, are discussed in Chapter 9.

THERAPY-SPECIFIC CHARACTERISTICS

Facilitative Conditions

Carl Rogers' (1957) proposal that the success of clinical encounters was dependent on clinician-proffered facilitative conditions consisting of accurate empathy, nonpossessive warmth, congruence, and unconditional positive regard has been the subject of considerable subsequent empirical investigation. The conclusion reached by the majority of these studies has been that a positive relationship exists between these clinician attributes and client therapeutic gain. However, a number of flaws have been found in these studies, and critics have suggested that the effect of these variables was inflated through the retrospective rating by clients of both therapy outcome and clinician attributes. This criticism has been muted somewhat by demonstration that independent ratings of clinician facilitative conditions are equally as predictive of outcome as client ratings (Beutler, Crago, & Arizmendi, 1986).

Social work studies of facilitative conditions have largely been evaluations of training programs to teach these skills, and as such are reported in Chapter 9. In a more general student survey, Jackson and Ahrons (1985) found no differences in emotional sensitivity levels between students pursuing clinical specializations and those in community organization specializations.

Psychotherapy studies have reported that levels of facilitative conditions vary by observer. A social work study investigated whether this divergence was also evident in empathy ratings of clinicians by clients, clinical colleagues, and clinicians themselves (Weeks, Kotsubo, Kamishita, Yokoyama, Cross, & Fischer, 1977). Results found no significant divergence; instead, considerable convergence between ratings was observed. Although these results are encouraging, caution is necessary in generalizing them due to the small sample size of the study.

Facilitative conditions can be considered independent clinician attributes or can be considered a product of the client-clinician relationship with both partners contributing equally to obtain a facilitative process. Conceptualized in the latter fashion, the joining of client and clinician inputs has been termed a *therapeutic alliance,* and as such has been studied. Results have demonstrated that a positive alliance contributes to positive clinical out comes. Furthermore, clients who were not predisposed to initial positive alliances with their clinicians could be influenced into a more positive alliance through direct confrontation of defensiveness, fear, and negative patterns of relating (Beutler et al., 1986). The importance of a therapeutic alliance in social work also has been discussed by Marziali (1988), who cited medical research involving social workers.

Expectations

The term expectations has been used to encompass a broad range of attitudes, including attitudes toward the structure of the clinical process, appropriate behaviors of clients in the therapeutic relationship, and outcome of the process. This diversity in definition of expectation has mitigated against convergence of findings in this area. Furthermore, studies of clini cian expectations in psychotherapy reveal that they are highly susceptible to change, particularly as a function of continuing observation and contact with a client over time. The effects of clinician expectations on the outcome of therapeutic process, therefore, have not been conclusively demonstrated. However, discrepancies between client and clinician expectations, particu larly at the onset of therapy, have been associated with premature termina tion (Baekeland & Lundwall, 1975). Given the propensity for clinician expectations to change, it has been suggested that the flexibility of such expectations is what is important in producing clinical change (Beutler et al., 1986).

In social work research, studies of clinician expectations have been de scriptive in nature and have targeted specific populations for study. In Pratt's (1970) study of attitudes toward improving health and health practices of the poor, for example, a sizable minority of social workers (37%) reported pessimistic expectations, and pessimism was highest among the best edu cated, most knowledgeable, and most involved workers. Pratt attributed the pessimism largely to lack of external resources for improving the condition of the poor, but also related it to stereotypes about the poor, such as the poor having limited aspirations. Pessimistic expectations were also found in Segal's (1970) study of five social workers and their mentally disable clients. Social workers in this study underestimated both the current daily activities and the goals of their clients.

Pessimistic expectations with regard to preventing physical abuse and changing abusers' behavior were reported by public welfare and family service workers (Davis & Carlson, 1981). Social workers' attitudes were more pessimistic than those of police officers or judges. Family service workers also were most likely to hold women responsible for the abuse and to advocate couple counseling as a remedial action (Davis, 1984).

In a survey of professionals involved with child sexual abuse cases, Wilks and McCarthy (1986) found that mental health workers were significantly more pessimistic about the benefits of therapy than child welfare workers or law enforcement officers. However, both child welfare and mental health workers were less punitive than law enforcement officers, who favored incarceration or removal of the father from the situation.

It has been suggested that the pessimistic attitudes observed reflect realistic appraisals by clinicians about the benefits of interpersonal interventions in situations that are characterized by personal trauma or deficits. Clinicians experienced in working with disadvantaged clients are cognizant of the limitations of verbal interventions in overcoming deprivation or trauma. Other helping professionals, in contrast, may still perceive personal counseling as a panacea for all ills. It should, furthermore, be noted that even though pessimistic expectations have been documented in several studies, there is no evidence that these attitudes affect clinical outcome.

Training and Experience

Differentiating the effects of experience or amount of client contact from level of training has been difficult in both psychotherapy and social work research. Training and experience tend to be highly correlated; social work training typically includes client contact and often is interspersed with periods of employment in the field.

In psychotherapy research, statistical controls and meta-analyses have been used to isolate the effects of experience. Results have indicated that experience was most likely to emerge as a positive factor when treatment involved difficult clients, when intensive and complex procedures were required, and when evaluations were made early in treatment and included drop-out rates (Beutler et al., 1986).

Social work studies have been less successful in isolating effects of training and experience because investigators frequently have constructed one variable that included both training and experience. Feldman and

Caplinger (1977), in a comparison of group work intervention, for example, defined experienced clinicians as senior master's degree (MSW) students and inexperienced clinicians as undergraduate students with no social work training or experience. Their results significantly favored the experienced group leaders, whose clients evidenced increased prosocial group behavior and decreased drop-out rates.

Several studies have focused on the effects of training. Rosen and Liberman (1972) found that trained workers, defined as MSW graduates, provided clients with more congruent responses than untrained workers, who were in-service trained workers. Untrained workers had particularly high levels of incongruent and retaliatory responses when faced with aggressive clients.

Evaluations of the deployment of social workers by level of training have failed to demonstrate consistent differences. Two studies have investigated the deployment of BSW and MSW social workers in hospital settings. Taggart (1982) found that BSW-level social workers were increasingly employed in clinical positions that had traditionally been defined as MSW-level positions, but that their employment did not result in any decrement of performance evaluation. Similarly a study of task performance and attitudes of hospital social workers failed to document significant differences between BSW- and MSW-level workers. The level of academic training appeared to be less significant than the difference between some academic training and none (Wattenberg & O'Rourke, 1978). However, these evaluations may not have been adequately sensitive to the differences between training levels.

Investigations of client-rated outcome have failed to document significant effects of either training or education. Beck's (1987) study of family service clients found only a nonsignificant trend that favored increased clinician education in helping clients with family-relations problems. However, this finding was balanced by a similar nonsignificant trend in the opposite direction that favored less educated clinicians in helping clients with other types of problems. The results of client evaluations were mirrored in drop-out rates. All of the workers in this study had at least bachelor-level training, and the author suggested that clinicians with lower levels of training may be more appropriate for clients with practical or environmental problems than clinicians with higher levels of training. Again, however, these differences were not statistically significant, and therefore, levels of academic training cannot be considered a major determinant in client outcome.

Style

Characteristics of clinician style that have been studied in psychotherapy investigations include therapist directiveness and self-disclosure. In both instances, although most consistently documented in relation to directiveness, the effects of clinician attributes were found to depend on complementarity with client attributes. As noted in the previous chapter, clinician directiveness produced positive results with externally controlled clients, whereas nondirectiveness was most effective with internally controlled clients. These results were confirmed in a study of parole officers and adolescent offenders that documented positive findings when officer directiveness was matched with offender characteristics (Palmer, 1973). Officers categorized as relationship/self-expression-oriented interacted best with independent, expressive offenders, whereas officers characterized as surveillance/self-oriented interacted best with anxious, dependent offenders.

Clinician self-disclosure, which has demonstrated positive effects in analogue studies, has produced mixed effects in clinical trials, suggesting again the possibility of interaction with client attributes (Beutler et al., 1986). Two social work studies have investigated the effects of clinician self-disclosure. Bradmiller (1978) found low levels of clinician disclosures to clients among social workers. The amount of disclosure was found to vary with clinician marital status; married clinicians disclosed more than unmarried clinicians. Bradmiller speculated that this might be due to the greater breadth of personal experience in disclosure available to married clinicians. Anderson and Mandell (1989) studied 160 Oregon social workers and found a higher level of clinician disclosure to clients than the earlier Bradmiller (1978) study. The authors suggested that clinicians had become more aware of the benefits of disclosure in the intervening decade and hence were more prone to utilize it in their practice. Anderson and Mandell did not find the association between marital status and disclosure reported by Bradmiller, but did find an association with clinician theoretical orientation. Psychodynamic clinicians were found to disclose significantly less than clinicians of other orientations. Studies of the effect of self-disclosure on client outcome have not been reported in the social work literature.

Theoretical Orientation

Psychotherapy reviews have concluded that the effect of theoretical orientation on clinical outcome is largely negligible, with the exception of cognitive and behavioral orientations, which have been observed to produce the largest size effects over the broadest array of problems (Beutler et al.,

1986). However, the suggestion has repeatedly been made that greater refinement in the study of theoretical orientations is necessary, in that different orientations are likely to have different impacts given different client types and problems. This kind of investigation, while still in its infancy, has been strongly recommended.

Studies of the effects of theoretical orientations in social work typically have been descriptive, reporting the distribution of social workers who identify with various theoretical schools. This identification has been found to be a function of the era in which professional training was received; social workers trained in the 1960s identified primarily with psychoanalytic ego psychology, while those trained in the 1970s identified more with systems theory (Mackey, Burdek, & Charkoudion, 1987). Other studies have suggested that social workers typically do not identify with any one theoretical orientation, but consider themselves eclectic, using parts of many different orientations (Jayaratne, 1978, 1982). Furthermore, the relationship between theoretical orientations espoused by clinicians and clinical action may be negligible. A study of theoretical orientations and proposed clinical actions in response to client analogues found only weak associations between these variables (Kolevzon & Maykranz, 1982).

A comprehensive analysis of theoretical orientations and hypothetical clinical behavior of social workers was reported by Cocozelli (1986, 1987) and Cocozelli and Constable (1985). Reported results indicated that 90% of the clinical social workers surveyed claimed to have been influenced by authors of either the explanatory type, defined as psychoanalytic, psychosocial, or ego psychology, or by the interactional type, defined as family therapy or systems theory. However, neither clinical beliefs about practice nor hypothesized behavior were influenced directly by these orientations. The best predictor of clinical behavior was the type of problem presented, with 40% to 60% of the within subject variation explained by this variable. In contrast, only 4% to 12% of between groups variation was explained by professed orientation. Within theoretical orientations, more than 60% of variance can be explained by one dimension representing an action-interactional versus a reflective-individual continuum. Cocozelli (1986) concluded that social work behavior was largely dependent on client needs. Clinicians responded to these needs with unique experientially based paradigms, which were only somewhat related to theoretical influences. These conclusions, however, must be constrained by the nature of the study in that vignettes summarizing client attributes and problems rather than actual client presentations were used.

The association between theoretical orientation and clinician attitudes toward women was investigated by Davenport and Reims (1978), who failed to find any significant association of these variables, but found instead that attitudes toward women differed by clinician sex. Male clinicians had more conservative attitudes than female clinicians.

Vendorship

As social work services have become increasingly privatized in North America, concern has been voiced about the extent and effect of private delivery of social work services. The primary concerns have been that, as social work services move into the marketplace, the traditional focus on providing services to the disadvantaged will be eroded because social workers will identify themselves more as therapists than social workers and be less connected with the community social service delivery network.

Studies that have investigated the differences between agency and private practice social workers have reported mixed results. In a comparison of agency and private practice social workers in Los Angeles, Borenzweig (1981) found that agency clinicians were more likely to provide services to the poor, children, and psychotics than private clinicians who served primarily the middle class, young adults, and neurotics. Agency clinicians were also more likely to refer clients to community resources and less likely to use traditional psychotherapeutic techniques. No differences in professional affiliations, however, were observed. Grosser and Block (1983), in contrast, found in a survey of 948 Colorado mental health clinicians that private practitioners were providing a range of services not dissimilar to services provided by clinicians in the public sector. A study of Massachusetts social workers comparing social work practice before and after the passage of a state law granting social workers vendor status found no major changes in the delivery of services, except for an increase of independent operations by social workers as compared to previous associate practices with other professionals (Shatkin, Frisman, & McGuire, 1986).

Clinician satisfaction with private practice has been the subject of several nationwide surveys. Wallace (1982) reported a 1975 survey of NASW private practitioners that found high levels of satisfaction with this type of practice. A repeat survey of NASW members in 1985, reported by Jayaratne, Siefert, and Chess (1988), confirmed high job satisfaction levels among private practitioners and found it was significantly higher than levels reported by agency clinicians. Private practitioners reported a higher level of congruence between their expectations of practice and their current activities, while public service clinicians reported high levels of underutilization of skills and expertise. Private practitioners were found to be more experienced and to earn greater incomes than their agency counterparts. Comparing their results with the earlier 1975 survey, the authors concluded that the number of social workers in full-time private practice had increased more than fivefold over the past decade. In 1985 more than one-third of NASW members were engaged in some type of private practice.

A similar discussion of vendorship in relation to social workers in medical settings has focused on service delivery in Health Maintenance Organizations (HMOs), or voluntary prepaid health organizations. Two studies of social work activities in these settings have indicated that at least three-quarters of social work activity was devoted to direct clinical services of a psychotherapeutic nature (Mayer & Rubin, 1983; Poole & Braja, 1984). Whether these results indicate an overly restrictive definition of social work practice, which is contrary to the traditional psychosocial perspective, has been debated.

SUMMARY

In social work practice, as in psychotherapy, extratherapy clinician attributes, such as age, sex, ethnicity, and socio-economic status, have been found to exert minimal effects on the clinical process and to be of less relevance than other variables such as client problems. Clinician attributes, when considered alone, have had little effect on clinical outcomes. Clinician-client matching on such attributes has been found to exert a greater influence. The effects of matching, however, may be either positive or negative, depending on the nature of the client problem and/or client attributes. Further study of matching that is client- and problem-specific is necessary.

The study of therapy-specific characteristics in psychotherapy studies has yielded more positive results. In social work studies, however, these characteristics have been studied infrequently in relation to outcome. Results regarding the effects on clinical outcome of characteristics such as clinician training and experience have been mixed.

The theoretical orientations of clinical social workers, like those of psychotherapists generally, have been found to be eclectic. Not only do clinicians espouse a number of theoretical orientations, but the approaches they use in practice tend to vary by client problems. Clinical social workers appear to be sensitive to the needs of clients and flexible in their approaches to client problems, striving to tailor the intervention to the problem. In general, the studies of clinician characteristics point to the need to consider these factors in the context of client problems and types. The effects of clinician attributes are most likely to be discerned in association with specific client problems and characteristics. Further studies of this nature are necessary to understand the impact of clinician attributes on clinical outcome.

Chapter 4

CLINICAL ENVIRONMENTS

The rationale for studying clinical environments has been based on the assumption that negative environmental factors that impinge on clinicians in turn result in negative client-clinician interactions and outcome. The question of interest to researchers has been whether this assumption is true. In terms of clinical research in social work, however, only the first part of the equation, the effect of clinical environment on clinicians, has been subjected to substantial inquiry. The larger question has been addressed only in a limited manner.

In social work, clinical environments have received more attention in administrative than in clinical research (Blau, 1960; Kermish & Kushin, 1969). Administrative concerns, such as job turnover and productivity, have promoted investigation of factors influencing clinician job satisfaction and burnout. Clinical researchers have paid less attention to the clinical environment, perhaps due to lack of interest in what are seen to be managerial concerns or a perceived lack of control over environmental factors. Given the assumption that environmental factors, through the mediating influence of the clinician, affect client outcome, however, the necessity of exploring these factors becomes obvious.

In social work research, both negative and positive effects of clinical environments have been investigated. Negative effects of such factors as stress, job dissatisfaction, and burnout have been the focus of most studies. More positively, interventions to remedy negative environmental factors have been studied. In addition, the hypothesized positive buffering effects of environmental supports, such as clinical supervision, have been investigated.

The study of environmental factors has been hampered by a lack of conceptual clarity, in definition of both concepts and the relationships between concepts. Concepts such as stress, for example, have been given multiple definitions, have been interchangeably defined as independent and dependent variables, and have been investigated in terms of correlations with other factors without determination of the directionality of effects. In order to proceed with a review of factors in clinical environments, a clarification of definitions is necessary.

DEFINITION OF CONCEPTS

Maslach (1982, 1987) noted the lack of conceptual clarity in the psychological discussions of clinical environments and proposed both theoretical and operational definitions to differentiate concepts of job satisfaction, burnout, and stress. Lack of clarity has been equally evident in the social work literature in which concepts such as stress, tedium, burnout, and job satisfaction have been used interchangeably or as overlapping concepts without articulation of differences.

Maslach noted that studies of clinical environments often investigate a diversity of variables without providing an adequate theoretical rationale for linking or differentiating between them. The following discussion of job satisfaction, burnout, and stress presents the range of definitions used in social work studies for each of the terms.

Job satisfaction, according to Jayaratne and Chess (1983), has been better defined than stress and burnout in that it has been defined primarily as a function of environmental factors in the work setting. Job comfort, job challenge, financial rewards, opportunity for promotion, role ambiguity, role conflict, and work load have been the primary factors considered as components of job satisfaction. Jayaratne and Chess pointed out that the more evolved definition of job satisfaction may reflect its longer research history. In spite of this history, there are few studies of job satisfaction in clinical social work. Burnout, a more recent and less well-defined concept, has generated numerous studies. This may be due, in part, to the more clinical nature of the burnout concept.

Burnout, according to Maslach's (1982) definition, is a much more limited concept than job satisfaction, denoting a specific syndrome of emotional exhaustion, depersonalization, and reduced personal accomplishment that occurs in response to a specific environmental stressor, namely, "the chronic emotional strain of dealing with (troubled) human beings." The Maslach Burnout Inventory, based on this definition, has been the measure most widely used in the study of burnout (Maslach & Jackson, 1981). The subscales of the measure have low intercorrelations, indicating that the three factors make separate contributions to the concept of burnout. Several other definitions of burnout and measures of burnout exist, but typically they refer to one or two factors in the Maslach definition (Shinn, 1982).

Stress has been the least consistently defined concept in this area. It has been used indiscriminately to refer either to overwhelming environmental forces or stressors or to the effects of these factors on individual functioning (Donovan, 1987). Furthermore, stress, as a reaction, has at times been used synonymously with both job dissatisfaction and burnout. In addition, physical symptoms that are considered to be work related have been incorporated into several stress measures (Shinn, 1982). Since most social work studies have investigated the correlation of stress with job satisfaction or burnout, or used stress as a synonym for these variables, studies on stress will be discussed in the context of job satisfaction and burnout.

The present review uses Jayaratne & Chess' (1983) definition of job satisfaction and Maslach's definition of burnout as different, but somewhat overlapping, reactions to environmental stressors. Studies are categorized in terms of the nature of the measures used, which tend to be more definitive than the actual terminology used by the authors.

JOB SATISFACTION

Client Outcome

Job satisfaction has been considered to be a factor in clinicians' intent to change jobs, or job turnover, and hence to indirectly affect client outcome. Turnover results in discontinuity of service, and evidence exists that continuity is a factor in client satisfaction with service and in treatment compliance (Breslau, 1982; Russell, James & Berlow, 1987). The direct link between job satisfaction, continuity, and client outcome has not, however, been investigated.

Jayaratne & Chess (1983) studied the correlation between job satisfaction and intent to change jobs in their survey of 533 randomly selected NASW members and found that, although there was an inverse correlation between job satisfaction and intent to change jobs ($r = -.58$), only 26% of the variance in job change intent was explained by the job factors studied. They concluded that other factors, such as opportunity, played a more significant role in predicting job discontinuance. In a subsequent re-analysis of the same data, Jayaratne & Chess (1986) reported a significant trend for younger caseworkers to be both more dissatisfied and more likely to seek job change. They speculated that when job dissatisfaction coexisted with decreased employment opportunities negative effects such as clinician burnout could be expected to ensue.

Shinn (1982) reviewed the job satisfaction literature to determine the extent of association between job satisfaction and job turnover and found that only 15% of the variance in job turnover decisions could be attributed to job satisfaction levels. The conclusion that job satisfaction was only a minor factor in job change decisions and that other factors contributed more significantly to such decisions was supported.

In a more direct investigation of the effects of job satisfaction on clinical activity, Berg (1980) investigated the correlation of job satisfaction levels with the intake decisions of 42 social workers in a juvenile court setting. Results indicated that a very small proportion of the variance in decision-making was attributable to level of worker satisfaction and that only in relation to male clients. Client sex and race were considerably more powerful predictors of the types of decisions made. Berg concluded, however, that even if effects of job satisfaction were minimal, they deserved serious consideration because the clinical decisions made had long-term client consequences.

The reverse hypothesis, namely that client factors influence clinician job satisfaction, has been investigated in several studies. In a study of social workers providing services to the terminally ill, Parry & Smith (1988) found that under conditions of optimal client care, defined in this setting as client symptom control, clinicians reported higher levels of satisfaction than when care was less than optimal. Buffum and Konick (1982) similarly found clinician job satisfaction in a residential psychiatric setting was associated with the functional level of residents. Satisfaction was not associated with improvement in residents' level of functioning, however, except when discharge to community facilities was considered. The authors suggested that clinicians responded positively to the concrete evidence that the residents were ready for discharge, rather than to the less concrete evidence of improving daily ward behavior.

Most of the social work research on job satisfaction has been descriptive, associating satisfaction levels with variables of work settings, gender, and age.

Agency Setting

A number of surveys that compared levels of job satisfaction across agency settings did not find differences between settings, reporting generally high job satisfaction levels in all settings (Jayaratne & Chess, 1984; Sze & Ivker, 1986; Ullman, Goss, Davis, & Mushinski, 1971).

Jayaratne and Chess (1984) found that overall satisfaction levels and intent to change jobs did not differ by setting. Some variability in perceptions of working environments, however, was observed; child welfare workers reported higher levels of depersonalization, role ambiguity, and role and value conflicts than family service or mental health workers. Job challenge and comfort were reported to be highest among family service workers, lower among mental health workers, and lowest among child welfare workers. Dissatisfaction among child welfare workers was also found by Harrison (1980), who reported lower satisfaction levels in this population than a comparative NASW sample. Sze and Ivker (1986) in their nationwide survey of 686 social workers found uniformly high satisfaction levels across settings but found that job-related symptoms of stress varied by setting: Hospital workers reported the highest proportion of symptoms (14%); university personnel reported the lowest (5%). Hospital social workers and social workers in other settings, however, were found to have equivalently high satisfaction levels in an earlier survey (Ullman, Goss, Davis, & Mushinski, 1971).

In summary, very little variability in job satisfaction has been observed between agency settings. Social workers in private practice, however, have tended to report consistently higher levels of satisfaction than agency-employed workers (Jayaratne, Siefert, & Chess, 1988; Wallace, 1982).

To determine the facets of social work jobs that correlated with job satisfaction, Jayaratne and Chess (1983) conducted a nationwide survey of NASW social workers. Results indicated that the previously identified variables of job comfort, challenge, financial reward, promotion, role ambiguity, and role conflict were all found to be related to job satisfaction. Job challenge was the most significant predictor, accounting for 36% of job satisfaction variance. Work load was the only factor in their model that did *not* correlate with job satisfaction. In a comparison of workers in different settings, the most significant common predictor of job satisfaction was promotional opportunities.

A survey of clinical social workers that asked whether they would choose to train as social workers again if they were starting over found that this choice was related to workers' perceptions of the status of the profession

(Reiter, 1980). Workers who rated social work as having a high status were more likely to choose it again. Income was not significantly associated with this choice.

Teamwork is a job facet that has been singled out for study in psychiatric settings and found to correlate with worker satisfaction (Toseland, Palmer-Ganeles, & Chapman, 1986). In spite of frequent grumbling about teamwork, most social workers endorsed the statement that teams improved treatment planning and service delivery to clients.

Clinician Characteristics

Gender

Differences in job satisfaction by clinician gender have been investigated primarily among social work managers with the fairly consistent finding that female managers are less satisfied with their jobs than male managers (Haynes, 1983; Jayaratne & Chess, 1986). Haynes found that the primary correlate of lower female job satisfaction levels was a perception that supervisors lacked confidence in female managers. Haynes attributed this to female managers' lack of preparation in dealing with administrators and their unrealistic expectations of administrators. The alternate explanation, that negative attitudes exist toward female managers, was not discussed but would seem to be equally plausible.

Age

Differences in job satisfaction by age reported by Jayaratne and Chess (1986) prompted some concern that new workers entering the field were finding social work intrinsically less satisfying. However, whether this dissatisfaction was unique to social workers or typical of all young people entering the labor market was not discussed.

In summary, surveys of social workers' satisfaction with their work settings generally have indicated high levels of satisfaction, which vary somewhat by type of setting, gender, and age. While job dissatisfaction has been suggested to result in higher rates of job change and increased service discontinuity or, alternately, thwarted job change intentions and burnout, these associations have yet to be empirically demonstrated.

BURNOUT

In contrast to job satisfaction, which has been investigated primarily in terms of environmental correlates, burnout has been studied in terms of psychological, environmental, and demographic factors. Also, while job dissatisfaction has been defined primarily in terms of cognitive appraisal, burnout has been defined as a complex and evolving psychological reaction. According to Maslach's (1982) definition, burnout progresses through stages of *emotional exhaustion*, or being overwhelmed by emotional demands imposed by others; *depersonalization*, or development of a detached, callous, and dehumanizing response to others; and finally to a feeling of *reduced personal accomplishment*, or sense of inadequacy to help others. These reactions are assumed to have a direct effect on client service, producing less effective service to clients and poorer client outcomes.

Client Outcome

As with job satisfaction, the question of importance in relation to burnout is whether clinician burnout has any effect on client service. While extreme levels of burnout are considered, by definition, to be disabling, the effect of the more commonly observed low-to-moderate burnout levels on client service requires examination. Only a few studies have directly investigated client consequences of clinician burnout.

Beck's (1987a) survey of 17 family service agencies, which yielded responses from 244 clinicians and 1,617 clients, investigated the correlation of clinician burnout and client outcome. Clinicians in these agencies typically reported low burnout levels, and the effects on client outcome were minimal. Burnout levels were not found to correlate with outcome measures, such as client change, client satisfaction, or ratings of clinician-client relationships. The only client outcome measure that correlated with clinician burnout was drop-out, or premature termination, and this association was statistically significant only when clinicians of clients who dropped out were contrasted to clinicians of clients with all other types of terminations. Furthermore, the correlation failed to establish whether the greater number of clients terminating prematurely was what led to clinicians' negative self-appraisal and burnout, or whether burned-out clinicians were less likely to effectively engage clients.

Corcoran's (1987) study of 88 female NASW members from Texas purported to demonstrate the effects of burnout on clinician perceptions of clients. Negative perceptions of clients were found to correlate with burnout scores in a statistically significant manner. However, the magnitude of the correlations was low, ranging from $r = .23$ to $r = .34$, and probably was due to the fact that the depersonalization scale on the burnout inventory used was essentially a measure of negative attitudes toward clients. Furthermore, there was no evidence that these negative attitudes were actually reflected in clinician-client interactions or had any effect on client outcomes.

In short, evidence that clinician burnout affects client outcome is meager, at best. Clients to date have not reported less satisfaction with service or less favorable subjective evaluations of outcome when the service was provided by clinicians with higher burnout levels. The evidence that clinicians themselves differentially experience burnout symptoms, however, has received more empirical support.

Competence, Ability, and Sense of Accomplishment

Lack of a sense of accomplishment and evidence of therapeutic success was identified as the primary factor in burnout in Ratliff's (1988) review of burnout studies. In one survey of psychotherapists, for example, 74% cited lack of therapeutic success as the single most stressful aspect of clinical work. Social workers, more than any other professionals, cited personal depletion, or physical and emotional exhaustion, as a problem (Farber & Heifetz, 1982). While Ratliff's review included all helping professionals and did not distinguish among job dissatisfaction, stress, and burnout, several social work studies have specifically investigated the relationship between self-perceptions of competence and burnout.

Streepy (1981), using a measure of burnout constructed of 13 items related to stress-related symptoms and attitudes toward clients, found that social workers who reported difficulty in providing service to clients because of lack of skills and knowledge reported higher levels of burnout than workers who felt more able to cope with the job. Beck's (1987a) survey of family service workers reported similar findings, including a significant correlation between burnout and workers' perception of being handicapped in providing services because of lack of skills and knowledge.

Difficulties inherent in determining client progress were considered by Ratliff to contribute to burnout among helping professionals. Difficulties in determining expected rates of change, appropriate termination criteria, and lack of feedback from clients all were considered to contribute to clinicians' low sense of efficacy and high job satisfaction. While Ratliff did not associate these negative perceptions with deficits in training or lack of knowledge about effective helping methods, it would seem that both more comprehensive training and more emphasis on clinical research would lead to more realistic clinical expectations as well as development of specific criteria for evaluating client progress. Support for the effects of training on burnout are presented in the section on burnout interventions.

Job Facets Related to Burnout

Because burnout overlaps with the concept of job dissatisfaction, it is not surprising that various job facets have been found to correlate with burnout. Two studies have investigated these correlations among populations of family service workers. Dissatisfaction with job rewards, including salary, promotional opportunities, and hours of work, were found to be predictive of burnout in Beck's (1987a) survey. Work pressure, or pressure to increase output and threats to job security, were found to correlate with burnout by Streepy (1981). The perception that caseload size was excessive was found to be correlated with burnout by Beck, but *no* correlation was found between actual caseload size or hours of client contact and burnout. Dissatisfaction with job importance and job autonomy were also reported by Beck to correlate with burnout.

The extent to which working with the terminally ill results in burnout was investigated in a survey of personnel in 40 hospice settings (Mor & Laliberte, 1984). In spite of the difficulties of working with this client group, rates of reported burnout were low. Social workers and nurses, however, reported higher levels of emotional exhaustion and depersonalization than other staff members. A correlation was observed between perception of support from the hospice's interdisciplinary team and level of reported burnout, suggesting that internal support systems might be effective in reducing or preventing burnout.

Clinician Characteristics

Self-Esteem

Clinician characteristics have been investigated in terms of their association with burnout, but since these studies were correlational, the direction of the influence has not been determined. Correlations of burnout with self-esteem have been observed, suggesting either that burnout results in low self-esteem or, conversely, that individuals with low self-esteem are more prone to burnout (Caron, Corcoran, & Simcoe, 1983). LeCroy and Rank (1987) focused on a particular type of self-esteem, professional self-esteem, which they defined as the subjective evaluation regarding the prestige and perceived worth of social work coupled with the opportunities for personal growth, fulfillment, and service to others in the profession. They constructed a measure of the discrepancy between clinicians' perceived and ideal professional self-esteem. This measure was found to be the best independent predictor of burnout in their study.

Age

A negative correlation between age and burnout has been found in several studies of other helping professionals, but this finding has not been consistently replicated in social work studies. Beck (1987) found a small but statistically significant negative correlation between age and burnout in her study of family service workers ($r = -.23$). LeCroy and Rank (1987), using a considerably smaller sample, found no such correlation. The present evidence, therefore, offers only modest support for the premise that younger social workers have higher burnout levels.

Gender

The study of the relationship between gender and burnout among social workers likewise has yielded inconsistent results. Beck (1987) reported higher burnout levels in male clinicians in family service agencies, whereas LeCroy and Rank (1987) found that females reported significantly higher levels of emotional exhaustion and negative feelings toward clients than males. Studies of female social workers have identified absence of social support as a significant predictor of one aspect of burnout, emotional exhaustion (Himle, Jayaratne, & Chess, 1987). For female social workers, emotional support was found to be equally important whether it was provided by supervisors or spouses (Davis-Sacks, Jayaratne & Chess, 1985), and lack of spousal support was associated with higher marital dissatisfaction levels (Jayaratne, Chess, & Kunkel, 1986).

Locus of Control

External locus of control, or the sense that one has little control over one's destiny, has been studied and found to be directly associated with burnout (Caron, Corcoran, & Simcoe, 1983). A somewhat analogous concept, being hassled or bothered by the minor irritations of daily living, was investigated by Johnson & Stone (1987) and found to be a significant predictor of burnout. Whether feeling hassled is a symptom of burnout or a precursor to burnout has not been established.

Other Measures of Burnout

Pines and Kafry (1978) used the term *tedium* to refer to symptoms of physical, emotional, and attitudinal exhaustion. They developed a measure of tedium that consisted of self-ratings of being depressed, burned-out, run-down, tired, and not having a good day. In a survey of 129 social workers, Pines and Kafry found tedium to correlate negatively with job satisfaction and positively with desire to leave the job and with negative attitude toward clients. Tedium subsequently has been found to be highly correlated with lack of general life satisfaction (Shinn, 1982).

Gillespie (1982) developed a measure of burnout using descriptive statements of coping responses, such as joking about clients and avoiding clients. Based on an analysis of the measure's internal consistency, Gillespie suggested that there are two dimensions to the measure. The *active* component of burnout was defined in terms of behaviors clinicians instigated to remove themselves or distance themselves from clients, whereas the *passive* component consisted of psychological detachment from clients.

In summary, burnout levels among social workers, particularly in clinical settings such as family service and mental health agencies, have been found to be relatively low. Correlates of burnout have primarily been clinician self-evaluations of competence or ability to provide required services. Environmental factors such as job rewards and job pressures also have been found to be predictors of burnout, but the evidence suggests that the subjective appraisal, rather than absolute level, of these factors is associated with burnout.

Most studies of burnout have been correlational and hence inconclusive in sorting out cause-and-effect relationships. Courage and Williams (1987) suggested that further multidimensional investigations are necessary to understand the complex interrelationships among the various factors. Maslach (1987), however, suggested that longitudinal studies would be more productive in developing an understanding of the precipitants of burnout and their resultant effects. Additional understanding of burnout can also be derived from the study of burnout interventions.

Burnout interventions

In spite of the current rudimentary understanding of burnout, attempts have been made to decrease levels of burnout among social workers. Brown (1984) described a loosely structured mutual-help group that aimed to provide emotional support and problem solving among workers in a child protection agency. Although high levels of satisfaction were reported by participants, no decrease in burnout indices were found in a pre- versus postgroup comparison.

Corcoran and Bryce (1984), acting on the finding that burnout was related to a perceived skill deficit, compared the effect of different training formats on clinician burnout. Human relations training was compared with microtraining and with a no-training control group. Posttraining measures indicated that human relations training, which focused on affective traits, significantly decreased burnout. No decrease was observed from the more cognitively structured microtraining format in which maintenance of pretraining burnout levels was observed. The no-training control group showed an increase in burnout level.

In summary, one study demonstrated the effectiveness of training in lowering burnout levels, when training contained an affective component. However, the more widely touted notion of mutual support groups to prevent or decrease burnout (Maslach, 1982; Scully, 1983) was not supported in the single study cited. Single studies, however, cannot be regarded as conclusive, and replications are necessary to determine whether the results reported can be generalized to other situations or populations.

SUPERVISION AS A BURNOUT BUFFER

Social work supervision has been considered to provide both social support and clinical knowledge and hence to provide a buffering or moderating effect on work-related stress. Furthermore, supervision has been considered to have the potential to improve clinical outcome by improving the functioning of clinicians (Watson, 1973). Supportive supervision was the term coined by Kadushin (1985) to refer to the specific function of supervision that enabled workers to provide clients with more effective and efficient service. Supportive supervision, according to NASW standards, includes management of work-related stress and provision of assistance to staff in coping with such stress. Kadushin further described the goal of supportive supervision as increasing motivation and reinforcing workers' ego defenses and capacity to deal with job stresses, again with the aim of enabling clinicians to function effectively. While the supportive goal of supervision has been widely heralded, and the assumption that supportive supervision would result in better service to clients has been repeatedly reiterated, the investigation of the link between supervision and client outcome has only begun.

Supervision typically has been considered to have a positive effect on workers, primarily as a buffer or source of emotional support against negative environmental stressors (Jayaratne, Tripodi, & Chess, 1983). The suggestion that supervision can also be a source of negative stress, however, has also been made in several studies. Most social work studies have not investigated actual effects of supervision but instead have investigated links between clinicians' perceptions of their work and their perceptions of their supervisors.

Facets of Supervision Related to Burnout

Supervisors typically interact with clinical social workers for various purposes, including the provision of information, support, and administrative control. In order for the supervisor-supervisee relationship to be perceived as positive and supportive, some agreement about the functions of supervision, or congruence of perceptions, is necessary (Munson, 1983). Definitions of supervision have ranged from Lowy's (1983) single, "a learning and teaching process," to Kadushin's (1985) multifaceted conceptualization, which encompasses educational, administrative, and support functions. Several clinical studies have investigated levels of agreement between supervisors and supervisees regarding these functions.

Kadushin (1974) surveyed 469 supervisors and 384 supervisees listed in the NASW directory to obtain their perceptions of supervision. Asked to rank the various functions of supervision, both supervisors and supervisees rated teaching job functions and providing case consultation as the primary supervisory functions. Providing emotional support was perceived as a major function by less than 5% of supervisors and supervisees, whereas administrative functions were perceived as important by twice as many supervisees (11%) as supervisors (5.5%). Satisfaction with supervision was reported to be generally high.

Poertner and Rapp (1983), who surveyed 120 supervisors and 227 supervisees, also reported high agreement levels between supervisors and supervisees in ratings of supervisory tasks. Tasks rated as supportive included both discussion of problem cases and listening to staff concerns. These were assigned high frequency ratings by supervisees and supervisors alike. Russell, Lankford and Grinell (1983) reported, however, that supervisees in a Texas survey did not rank their supervisors highly on task-centered or people-centered functions. Comparative supervisor perceptions were not reported. Granvold (1978) surveying supervisors' self-perceptions found that supervisors considered themselves high on worker-centered functions but low on organizational or structural functions.

Shulman, Robinson, and Luckyj's (1981) survey of 109 supervisors and 671 workers found a high correlation between worker perceptions of supervisor behavior and ratings of supervisor helpfulness. Supervisors who provided high levels of emotional support through empathic responding, development of a supportive atmosphere, and understanding worker's feelings were also likely to be rated as helpful. However, since both ratings were provided by workers, it is not clear if the high correlations observed (ranging from $r = .74$ to $r = .77$) were a function of supervisor behavior or worker perception.

Cherniss and Egnatios (1978) studied 164 mental health clinicians and their 22 supervisors and found a high preference among workers for feeling-oriented supervisors, as opposed to authoritative or laissez-faire supervisors. Clinical self-confidence was found to correlate negatively with authoritarian supervision ($r = -.18$).

Several studies of student supervision have addressed the differential importance of teaching and supportive functions within supervision. Baker and Smith (1988) found that student comfort, presumably an index of emotional support, was the best predictor of student satisfaction with supervision. This was followed closely by supervisor knowledge of practice, presumably an index of the teaching function. Curiel and Rosenthal (1987) found supervisor ability to relate theory and practice, a teaching function, to be highly predictive of student satisfaction. Comparing student and supervisor ratings of supervision, Rutholz and Werk (1984) found that while supervisors emphasized cognitive-structuring, or teaching functions, students placed greater emphasis on developing autonomous practice.

Conceptualizing supervision as a developmental process that changes in response to developing supervisee capacities and needs can explain some of the differences in perceptions between supervisees and supervisors, who may differentially emphasize the various stages of the process in their responses. The concept of a developmental supervisory process has received some empirical support. Cherniss and Egnatios (1978) reported a trend among novice clinicians to report more clinical self-confidence when they were provided with didactic/consultative supervision. However, since only 11 subjects were studied, the trend failed to reach statistical significance. Stoltenberg, Pierce, and McNeill (1987), in a study of clinical and counseling psychology students, found that students preferred less structure and less direct feedback as they became more experienced. However, no change in the preference for support was reported. In a study of supervision of marriage counselors, Cross and Brown (1983) found that while students reported decreased supervision time devoted to structured educational experiences over time, the amount of emotional support received was perceived to increase.

In summary, the supportive function of supervision, in contrast to the educational function, does not appear to decrease over time as clinicians gain experience and may, in fact, increase. Whether this provision of support to clinicians buffers stress and improves clinician functioning, which in turn improves clinical outcomes, has received little study.

Supervision and Client Outcome

Two studies in the present review have attempted to determine the effect of supervision on clinical outcome. One study was based on supervisors of unspecified discipline in a counseling center; the other was based on Israeli social workers. Couchon and Bernard (1984) studied 55 supervisor-clinician-client triads in a counseling center to determine the most effective timing of supervisory sessions. The interval between supervisory sessions and client counseling was varied from two days to four hours. The number of approved counseling strategies, or those discussed during supervision, used by clinicians varied according to proximity of supervisory sessions with counseling. However, no differences in client satisfaction were observed. Neither were there observed differences in clinician satisfaction with either counseling or supervision.

Eisikovits, Meier, Guttmann, Shurka, and Levinstein (1986) surveyed 63 Israeli social workers regarding their perceptions of supervision and agency treatment environments. Significant correlations between clinician perceptions of supervision and perceptions of agency attitudes toward clients were found. Supervision that was perceived to contribute to clinicians' professional development was correlated with encouragement of client autonomy and innovative client interactions. High administrative skill in supervisors was correlated with emphasis on client case planning and encouragement of client expressiveness. High supervisory expectations were correlated with discouragement of client anger and frustration. However, because all data were based on clinician perceptions and the analysis was correlational, clinician factors, rather than supervisor or client factors, more likely accounted for the reported associations.

In summary, the assumption that supervision influences clinician performance, which in turn influences clinical outcome, has not yet been empirically demonstrated. The number of studies investigating this relationship has been extremely limited, and further study is warranted. Clinician satisfaction with supervision has been more extensively investigated.

Gender and Sex Role in Supervision

The effect of gender matching in supervisor-supervisee pairs on satisfaction with supervision has been the subject of a series of studies. Munson (1979), in a study of 42 social work students, found that students were generally more critical of female supervisors, regardless of student gender. Behling, Curtis, and Foster (1982) studied 276 social work students and, in contrast to Munson, found that female students with male supervisors were the most dissatisfied, whereas gender-matched pairs were the most satisfied with supervision. Thyer, Sowers-Hoag, and Love (1986), employing a retrospective analysis of student evaluation of supervision, reported superiority of gender-matched pairs, with the highest satisfaction reported among female pairs. The authors advised caution in interpreting these results, however, noting that the gender variable only accounted for 5% of the variance in satisfaction ratings.

In an effort to determine the elements in cross-gender ratings more specifically, Petty and Odewahn (1983) compared considerate supervisory behaviors, characterized to be part of a female sex-role, with initiating behaviors, considered to be part of a male sex-role. Consideration was defined as the extent to which mutual trust, respect for ideas, and consideration for feelings were conveyed by supervisors. Initiation was defined as the extent to which roles were defined toward goal attainment. Initiating behaviors were perceived most positively by gender-matched pairs, whereas considerate behaviors were valued equally by all. Resistance by male supervisees to female initiating behaviors was observed. Similarly resistance by female supervisees to male initiating behaviors was noted.

Given the continuing change in perceptions of appropriate sex-role behavior, and the increased attention given to this topic in social work training, current replication of these findings is necessary. Lack of perceived support by supervisees who have supervisors of opposite gender may be cause for concern if this trend has continued and if it has demonstrable effects on clinician performance and/or client service.

Negative Effects of Supervision

Maslach (1982) has suggested that since the supervisory role is, by definition, clinician focused and since supervisors are expected to maximize supervisee job performance, regardless of environmental constraints, the likelihood of negative supervision effects is considerable. Specifically, the tendency for supervisors in discussing difficult cases with supervisees to address the individual clinician's limitations, rather than institutional or situational factors, can be expected to reduce clinician perceptions of competence and job accomplishment. Evidence from clinical studies has tended to support this assertion.

Empirical evidence for the negative effects of supervision was provided by Wasserman's (1970) participant observation study of 12 newly graduated child welfare workers over a two-year period. During that time, half of the workers developed varying degrees of physical fatigue and emotional upset. Supervisors of these workers were perceived to provide neither support nor information that assisted workers in their job performance. At the end of the two-year period, three-quarters of the new recruits had left the agency.

Cherniss (1980) studied a range of human service professionals and found that professionals with the greatest amount of burnout generally worked under supervisors who were frequently unavailable and/or dictatorial and authoritative.

Munson (1981), studying 65 social work supervisor-supervisee pairs compared supervisee perceptions of supervisor authority with satisfaction levels. Supervisors perceived to derive their status from the authority or sanction of their positions, as opposed to their competence and expert knowledge, were assigned lower ratings of supervisee satisfaction. Furthermore supervisees of these authoritarian supervisors, who limited their interactions with supervisees to the task level and did not socialize or show personal concern for the supervisees, also reported lower levels of job satisfaction and personal accomplishment.

Negative effects of supervision were also reported in several of the gender-matched studies cited previously. In particular, negative effects were reported by female students supervised by male supervisors, who were perceived as encouraging competition with other students for grades, providing lower grades to their female students, and providing less time and attention to their female supervisees.

The demonstration of both positive and negative clinician-rated correlates of supervision cannot be taken to mean that supervision causes these effects. Clinicians who are unhappy with their jobs are likely to perceive their supervision negatively, along with most other aspects of their jobs. Similarly, clinicians who are happy in their positions are likely to perceive supervision in a positive light. No studies in the present review varied supervision systematically in terms of type, intensity, or duration to establish the effect of these variations on clinical outcome.

Supervision and the Buffering Hypothesis

The specific effect of supervision in buffering or mediating environmental stresses was investigated by Jayaratne, Tripodi, and Chess (1983). They defined stress as a composite of role ambiguity and role conflict and strain, or the result of environmental stressors. Supervisory support was hypothesized to be a moderating or intervening variable between such environmental stressors and clinician job satisfaction, depersonalization, and emotional exhaustion. The predicted negative correlations between supervisor support and emotional exhaustion were observed. However, in the evaluation of factors contributing to job stress, no evidence of the mediating or intervening effect of supervision was found. None of the partial correlations of support in the regression equations for role ambiguity or role conflict were significant. The authors concluded that support for the buffering hypothesis was lacking.

In summary, while there is evidence of an association between clinicians' perceptions of their jobs and their perceptions of their supervisors, the nature of this association remains undetermined. Several alternate explanations, namely, that supervisors mediate job-related stress, cause additional stress, are scapegoats for work-related stress, or suffer from the same environmental stressors as their supervisees, remain equally plausible. In contrast to the repeatedly articulated theoretical notion of supervision providing a buffer to job stress, empirical data suggest that, in some situations, supervision is associated with increased stress. Whether these increases are a function of supervisor behaviors or clinician factors, however, has not been determined. Nevertheless, further study of supervision needs to encompass negative as well as positive consequences of this process.

SUMMARY

Environmental factors in clinical settings have been found to influence clinicians' subjective evaluation of their jobs, their intention to change jobs, and their sense of emotional and physical well-being. The relationship of environmental factors to clinicians' job performance, or service to clients, however, has not been demonstrated. While it is evident that clinicians' perceptions of clients are affected by their perceptions of the work environment, there is little direct evidence that their behavior toward clients is altered as a result. The relationship of clinician burnout to client dropout is, at present, suggestive and warrants further investigation.

The primary limitation in studies of environmental factors has been their correlational nature. Little effort has been made to demonstrate cause-and-effect linkages. Longitudinal studies in which environmental factors are varied with subsequent monitoring of their effects on clinician behavior and client outcome are necessary. Only such investigations can test the assumptions and hypotheses that environmental factors significantly affect not only clinical social workers but also their clinical outcomes.

Chapter 5

THE CLINICAL PROCESS

Definitions of the clinical process in social work, that elusive essence of client-clinician interaction, have changed over time in both substance and specificity. Siporin (1983) summarized the evolution in definition as moving from a magical process connoting a mystique or cult to an empirical, behavioral delineation of stages and tasks. Rosen and Proctor (1979), in accord with the latter definition, referred to social work process as the interactive system jointly produced by client and clinician behavior.

A number of definitions have focused on the more concrete or structural aspects of process. Nelsen (1985), referring to the independent variable in clinical interaction, suggested that the clinical process could be understood in terms of form, content, dosage, and context. In the psychotherapy literature, Orlinsky and Howard (1978) suggested that process can be understood in terms of its behavioral, perceptual, symbolic, and normative aspects. More recently, elements of process were considered in terms of contract, interventions, bond, client self-relatedness, and therapeutic realizations (Orlinsky & Howard, 1986).

The definition used in this chapter of clinical process borrows from and extends the definitions above. Process is defined in terms of phases, beginning with entry and engagement, resulting in negotiation, communication, and adherence with clinician-initiated interventions and strategies.

Psychotherapy studies have examined clinical process primarily in relation to client outcome. In contrast, most social work research has remained at the descriptive level. Nevertheless, social work studies have provided considerable knowledge of the clinical process.

ENTRY AND ENGAGEMENT

Entry and engagement in the clinical process have been studied in terms of the decision to seek help, the sources of help contacted, and the referral process. Each of these areas will be considered in turn.

The Decision to Seek Help

In order for a client to become engaged in a helping process, several preliminary processes must have occurred. Client awareness of a problem or situation that is defined as atypical or distressing is a prerequisite to seeking help. Furthermore, clients must decide that assistance is required and must make decisions about the source of help to be sought out. Seeking help must be perceived as feasible and worthy of the cost and effort of doing so. Finally, contact with the help provider must be made.

The decision to seek help has been studied extensively in the medical literature. Marsh's (1980) review of this literature indicated that socio-economic factors were preeminent in making decisions regarding medical care. In addition, attitudinal factors have been found to be more important than symptomatology in making health care decisions (Ludwig & Gibson, 1969). Cultural factors also have been found to be significant determiners of illness behavior (Zola, 1966), and help-seeking has been found to correlate with a personality factor termed self-reliance (Phillips, 1965; Richard, 1975).

Help-seeking for psychosocial problems has been studied in relation to problems of domestic violence and addiction. In domestic violence situations, problem severity did not predict when or how help was sought; women who were assaulted by their husbands on a daily basis were less likely to seek help than women who were assaulted less frequently (Pahl, 1985). Similarly, in a comparative study of addicted and nonaddicted women, Marsh (1980) found that addiction did not predict help-seeking, whereas race and number of problems did. White women with many problems were the most likely to seek out formal sources of help. Black women, in contrast, tended to turn to informal sources of help. The importance of informal sources of help has been documented in many studies.

Sources of Help

Studies of sources of help for psychosocial problems have primarily compared informal sources, such as family and friends, with formal institutional or professional sources. These studies have indicated that family and friends are the most frequently contacted source of help, that they provide a much greater amount of help than social agencies, and that the level of satisfaction with this source of help is generally very high (Bowker, 1984; Pahl, 1985). Helping professionals were consulted primarily in situations when informal sources were not available, or when the help provided by these sources was judged to be insufficient.

Studies of decisions to seek help from social agencies have indicated that clients must overcome several barriers before they contact an agency. Studies of individuals with marital problems have indicated that women are twice as likely as men to seek outside help but that they do so reluctantly because they fear making their private problems public, are afraid of being disloyal to family members, and are uncertain about the reception they will receive (Borkowski, Murch, & Walker, 1983). Furthermore, individuals frequently have little knowledge of the services offered, have misconceptions about functions of social agencies, and fear the social control functions of such agencies. Prospective clients also have doubts about the competence of social workers to help them with life problems, expecting that social workers will be too young or too inexperienced to provide necessary help (Murch, 1980).

The study of barriers to engagement in the helping process has been limited to date but offers considerable potential for productive study. If early engagement in the clinical process is considered desirable, studying factors that inhibit engagement is the first step in dealing with those barriers.

The Referral Process

Client engagement with social workers, particularly those working in interdisciplinary settings, has traditionally been dependent on referrals from other professionals. The effectiveness of referral in providing optimal client service has been studied. Early studies of referrals to social workers in medical settings demonstrated that many referring agents had much narrower conceptions of social work services than social workers themselves did (Stockler, Sittler, & Davidson, 1966; Ullman & Kassebaum, 1961).

A number of studies have documented that clients who presented with psychosocial needs in medical settings frequently were not referred to social work. Healy (1981) found that only 61% of emergency room patients with urgent psychosocial needs received social services. Borland and Jones (1980) found that only 5% of patients in an outpatient clinic were referred for service, even though 38% of the patients reported psychosocial problems. In a pediatric clinic Soroker (1977) found that 34% of clients with psychosocial problems were referred to social work.

The most extensive studies of the referral process in social work were made by Berkman and Rehr (Berkman & Rehr, 1970; Gordon & Rehr, 1969). They found that medical staff referred clients for a restricted range of services, primarily discharge planning, and made referrals late in the period of hospitalization. When social workers did their own casefinding, client contact was earlier, more broadly defined, and more effective (Berkman & Rehr, 1973). Subsequent replications of these studies have confirmed that social work involvement in case identification results in earlier client contact in both medical (Boone, Coulton, & Keller, 1982) and psychiatric settings (Selig, 1978).

Inasmuch as referral to social work has been at least partly dependent on the role expectations of social workers held by other professionals, several studies have investigated this variable. Lister (1980) surveyed health professionals from 13 disciplines and found very low consensus on social work functions. However, the 36 tasks rated by physicians, nurses, physical therapists, hospital administrators, and medical technologists were selected to represent functions that could be carried out by more than one profession. Not surprisingly, the results indicated considerable overlap in perceptions of functions appropriate to any one professional group. Discharge planning tasks, however, were predominantly assigned to social workers. In another study, which utilized actual patient files, considerably greater consensus across professions was achieved in decisions regarding social work referral (Dove, Schneider, & Gitelson, 1985). Problems with ambulation and mental health were the criteria consistently used in making referrals to social work.

Rates of referral to social work have also been considered to vary by attitudes of medical personnel toward social work. Two studies that investigated physicians' attitudes toward social work referral both found that physicians were favorably disposed toward social workers and that they were quite prepared to refer patients with psychosocial problems to social workers (Gropper, 1988; Phillips, 1977).

In summary, studies of factors that inhibit clients from seeking help and factors that inhibit or promote interdisciplinary referrals have provided a beginning knowledge of the entry and engagement phase of the clinical process. Considerably more study is required so that this phase can be more fully understood, and social work clinicians can make use of this knowledge to provide services in a timely and effective manner.

CLINICAL ADHERENCE

Effective clinical intervention has commonly been assumed to rest on a continuous clinician-client relationship. Premature termination, discontinuance, or dropping out have been regarded as indicators of negative outcome. The terms clinical compliance and clinical adherence both have been used to denote client involvement in an acceptable course of treatment to produce a desired preventative or therapeutic result. Adherence is the preferred term because compliance potentially has negative connotations of client passivity and uninvolvement (Meichenbaum & Turk, 1987).

Client and Clinician Variables

Clinical adherence has been investigated extensively in the medical field, inasmuch as nonadherence has been considered to contribute to high health care costs. Rates of nonadherence to medical regimens as high as 92% have been reported, with rates typically ranging between 30% and 60% (Masek, 1982). Meichenbaum and Turk (1987) reviewed more than 200 variables that have been investigated in association with health care adherence and concluded that common stable client variables did not significantly predict adherence. Nevertheless, the majority of health care providers, particularly physicians, still attributed nonadherence to patient attitudes. The authors noted, however, that the lack of common client correlates with nonadherence does not preclude such a correlation in specific situations or in relation to specific problems. Furthermore, while no single client variable has been found to predict nonadherence, particular combinations of client variables may have predictive value. Gillum and Barsky (1974) suggested that patients who fail to admit the seriousness of their problems, doubt their own ability to comply, are hostile or aggressive, have poor social support and few social resources, and are required to follow complex regimens that require substantial life-style changes are most at risk for nonadherence.

In contrast to the lack of findings regarding client factors, several clinician factors have been found to correlate with adherence. Clinician variables such as attention to client speech, maintenance of eye contact, moderate levels of self-disclosure, and engaging clients in operationalizing treatment regimens all have been found to correlate positively with adherence in health settings (Meichenbaum & Turk, 1987).

In psychotherapy studies, nonadherence has been defined primarily in terms of drop-out or premature termination of treatment. Using these definitions, psychotherapy studies have likewise documented high nonadherence rates, with aggregate data suggesting that by the third interview 70% of clients were likely to have dropped out of treatment (Bakeland & Lundwall, 1975; Garfield, 1986; Phillips, 1985). Garfield (1986) concluded that, contrary to traditional expectations concerning length of therapy, most clients remained in therapy for only a few interviews. Furthermore, client expectations in entering treatment typically were that treatment would be short term and problem focused.

Client variables have not been found to be predictive of drop-out in psychotherapy, paralleling the findings of medical studies. Client age, sex, and diagnosis have not been found to correlate with drop-out rates. Some evidence exists that socio-economic status (SES) and race do predict drop-out, particularly when low SES nonwhite clients are paired with middle-class white clinicians (Garfield, 1986).

Few studies of clinical adherence in social work have been done in spite of the fact that client drop-out is a common phenomenon in interventions (Levy, 1987). Drop-outs from student caseloads were studied by Tolson and Brown (1981), who found a small but significant correlation between clinician skill level and client drop-out. Two studies that examined dropout from the client's perspective found that dropping out was not necessarily perceived as treatment failure by clients. Between 70% and 80% of clients who attended only one session and were considered by clinicians to have dropped out of service reported a degree of positive resolution of their problems (Presley, 1987; Toseland, 1987). These studies suggest that using clinician-generated definitions of drop-out may inflate rates of unsuccessful interventions.

Strategies to Increase Adherence

A number of strategies designed to increase the likelihood of adherence were reviewed by Levy (1987), and several social work studies have investigated the effects of these strategies. Gaines and Stedman (1981) found that self-referral, as opposed to referral by others, increased adherence rates in a family and children's service. Brigg and Mudd (1968) documented the benefits of phone-call reminders of appointments. Improving intake procedures by clarifying the services available for particular populations, such as maritally distressed women whose husbands refused counseling, multiple agency users, and violent couples, was found to significantly decrease drop-out in a family service agency (Russell, Lang, & Brett, 1987).

Other types of adherence, such as assigned-task completion, have not been studied systematically in social work research. However, as clinical social workers move toward greater specificity in interventions, this will become an increasingly important area for study.

NEGOTIATING CLINICAL CONTRACTS

Clinical adherence presupposes some agreement between client and clinician regarding the nature of the ensuing process. Reaching such an agreement typically follows a period of clarification or negotiation about the specifics of the process. The process of negotiation between client and clinician to establish a contract for social work intervention has been studied. Defining a contract as an explicit agreement between clinician and client on their present work and expectations of each other, Rhodes (1977) investigated the extent of clinician-client agreement among 15 client-clinician pairs. His study found moderately high agreement on most items. However, clients were found to desire greater direction, clinician friendship, more concrete advice, and shorter term interventions than clinicians. In a similar study of client perceptions and expectations, Lima, Eisenthal, and Lazare (1982) found a high degree of consensus between clients and clinicians. Significant differences were observed between clinicians and clients with regard to insight requests and limit setting. Clinicians consistently underestimated clients' expectations of, and desire for, insight and limit setting.

The actual process of clinical negotiation was studied by Kenmore (1987) in a qualitative study. Results indicated that clinicians moved from initially stating a position, to defending it against client opposition, and finally to altering it to meet client preferences. In a study of a slightly different type of contract—a contingency contract in which clients were rewarded for complying with therapeutic goals—Rose (1978) found that adults in assertiveness training groups were more likely to complete behavioral assignments when contracting was in place. However, in instances where participants felt negatively about contracting, the results of contract implementation also were negative.

In general, studies of the negotiating process have revealed moderate levels of appreciation of client expectations and wishes by clinicians. A consistent source of disagreement between clients and clinicians has been the duration or term of intervention. Research on this parameter of intervention has been reported in both psychotherapy and social work literature.

TERM AND DURATION OF INTERVENTION

Psychotherapy studies have investigated treatment duration in cases of both early termination and mutual termination. Garfield's (1986) review of psychotherapy studies revealed that, although the median length of treatment varied from 3 to 12 interviews, there was a clustering of terminations around 6 interviews. In the majority of studies, clients remained in treatment for only a few interviews; termination was not planned and was judged to be early and problematic by clinicians.

In relation to therapy outcome, the findings regarding duration appear somewhat contradictory. In studies that compared time-limited with unlimited therapy, Orlinsky and Howard (1986) noted that the results favored time-limited approaches. However, when duration of therapy and outcome was studied, the results generally indicated that clients who attended more sessions derived greater benefits. Two possible explanations of this contradiction were suggested. Clients in time-limited interventions frequently attended more sessions than clients in unlimited interventions, who tended to drop out after the fifth or sixth session. Furthermore, clinical improvement has been demonstrated to be proportionally greater in earlier sessions, with diminishing returns in subsequent sessions. Findings of psychotherapy studies thus support time-limited, short-term clinical interventions.

In social work investigations, duration of interventions has not been linked conclusively with outcome. Sainsbury, Nixon, and Phillips (1982) observed that clients involved in long-term casework frequently reported a loss of morale and frustration at the seeming aimlessness and endlessness of contacts. Beck and Jones (1973), in contrast, studying family service clients, found a positive correlation between duration and outcome. However, in the latter study, the average duration was seven interviews, indicating that most of the interventions studied were of a short-term nature.

Much of the research on short-term intervention in social work has been related to the task-centered approach developed by Reid and his associates (Reid, 1975, 1978; Reid & Epstein, 1977; Reid & Shyne, 1969;). A predetermined duration of eight sessions in this treatment approach resulted in outcomes equal to or better than interventions of unlimited or longer durations.

The criteria that social workers use to determine duration of treatment was the subject of a study by Fortune (1985). The number and type of problems presented by clients and client resources were found to be the primary criteria used in making this judgment. Short-term interventions typically were prescribed for clients with few problems or problems of an environmental, as opposed to an intrapsychic, nature. Furthermore, clients with greater ego strength, stronger motivation, lower anxiety, and stronger support systems were judged appropriate candidates for short-term interventions. Clinician factors were not associated with treatment duration preferences.

The effect of shortening the duration of individual interviews, rather than the total number of interviews, was investigated by Singh (1982). Sixty social workers in a large metropolitan psychiatric hospital utilized and then evaluated the brief interview approach. Although no comparison groups were used, positive outcomes in relation to client adjustment and ego strength were reported.

The processes in short-term or limited interventions have also been studied and found to differ from longer term interventions. The study of these processes has focused primarily on client-clinician communication patterns.

CLINICIAN-CLIENT COMMUNICATION

Communication processes in social work were studied extensively in the 1960s. This research along with subsequent studies was reviewed by Fortune (1981). Much of the early research was based on either Hollis's (1967) typology or the comparable typology of Reid (1967), which categorized clinician communications into reassurance, advice, exploration, confrontation, logical discussion, structuring, and clarifying intrapsychic or developmental causation. On the basis of her review, Fortune concluded that clinician communications consisted largely of reflection and exploration. Clinician experience was found to be a factor in explaining variability in technique utilization: Inexperienced clinicians were more likely to use exploration, whereas experienced clinicians were more likely to use techniques that promoted self-understanding. Client social class was also found to be a significant factor in determining communication type: Lower SES clients received more advice than middle-class clients.

The planned term of interventions was also found to influence clinician communication. Short-term interventions were found to contain less exploration and more influencing and structuring of communications by clinicians. Long-term interventions, in contrast, were found to contain more exploration and less structuring. These findings subsequently were confirmed in a study by Sucato (1978). Later studies used Reid's task-centered typology to describe clinician communications (Fortune, 1979b) or to correlate communications with outcome (Fortune, 1979a). In the latter study, communication among 24 client-clinician pairs indicated that clinicians who gave clients more direction or advice and clinicians who gave clients more explanation about their behavior tended to have better outcomes. A similar finding was reported by Blizinsky and Reid (1980), who found a significant correlation between the percentage of time devoted to specific presenting problems and the degree of problem change.

Advice or information giving was a factor observed to be positively correlated with outcome in the early studies reviewed by Fortune (1981). In a survey of 42 parents attending a youth guidance center (Ewalt and Kutz, 1976), the majority reported that they received advice from their clinicians and found it helpful. Even in cases where the advice was not followed, it was reported to be instrumental in stimulating thought about alternate modes of problem resolution.

Studies regarding the amount of advice offered by clinicians have reported contradictory findings. Proctor (1983), studying initial interviews, found low levels of advice giving by clinicians, whereas Kassel and Kane (1980), studying self-reports of clinicians about advice giving generally, reported high levels of advice giving by clinicians. The timing of advice giving appears to be an important variable, with advice given in early sessions less likely to be helpful than advice given in later sessions (Ewalt & Kutz, 1976).

Timing was also found to be a relevant variable in determining the correspondence between clinicians' intent to use various communication strategies and their actual use. Rosen and Mutschler (1982a), using an expanded classification system of 14 types of communication, found that clinicians were more accurate in predicting their use of techniques in early and late phases of intervention than in the middle phases of the clinical process. The authors attributed this finding to the greater complexity of the middle or working phase in clinical interventions.

The nature of clinician communications has been considered a function of client presentation, and this has been the topic of two studies. In a study of 40 interviews by two clinicians, Cunningham (1978) reported that clinicians' supportive communication increased in response to reflective, as opposed to instrumental, client communications. Mutschler and Rosen (1977) likewise found that clinicians responded affectively in a more positive manner when clients presented relevant, as opposed to irrelevant, content.

In summary, studies of clinical communication have provided significant insights into the processes that actually occur in interventions and the processes that are linked with positive outcome. Advice or information giving, for example, has consistently been evaluated as beneficial by clients. Further study of other types of communication and their association with outcome is clearly warranted.

Clinician communication or skill also has been studied in specific models of practice. Three models relevant to social work practice are reviewed below.

The Mediating Model

Shulman (1978, 1981) developed a system for analyzing social work practice based on an interactional or mediating perspective in which clinician behaviors were viewed as providing input, encouragement, and guidance as well as response to client actions and/or behaviors. Initially, 27 clinician skills were identified, some of which were specific to the beginning or end of the process, while others described external contacts. These skills were subsequently translated into observational categories that could be scored from videotapes by external raters. The resulting category observation system consisted of 10 categories.

Categories were considered to include both positive or *in-mode* behaviors and negative or *out-of-mode* clinician behaviors, Out-of-mode behaviors, which were considered to be nonproductive, included three categories: behaviors that directed the flow of work away from the theme of concern, clinician criticism of client behavior or feelings, and the provision of solutions. Shulman (1981) reported that 40% of clinician behavior was of this nature. In-mode behavior, in contrast, was productive behavior whereby clinicians behaved in a manner congruent with client concerns. A total of 49% of clinician behavior was of this nature. The remaining 10% was devoted to silence. The in-mode behaviors most frequently demonstrated by the clinicians were elaboration of theme of concern, reaching for feelings, and providing data. Three skills were used less than 1% of the time by clinicians: clarification of purpose, making a demand for work, and identifying obstacles to productive work.

This system of studying clinical process had several benefits: The system of categories was based on social work theory and applied specifically to social work practice; it used an observational system rather than relying on self-reports by clinicians or clients, which have high potential for bias, and it attempted to capture the reciprocal nature of client-clinician interaction.

Shulman (1981) also identified worker communication skills and correlated them with client reports of helpfulness of service. The skills found to correlate most highly with client perceptions of clinician helpfulness were skills related to clinician empathy, specifically clinicians' ability to put clients' feelings into words and to understand clients' feelings.

Shulman's study of the clinical process made a significant contribution to the understanding of social work interventions. The development of a category observation system, in particular, provided a direct and useful way of studying this process. It is a method that warrants further attention.

Family Intervention Strategies

Family interventions, based on a wide range of theories and assumptions, are frequently used by clinical social workers. The extent of commonality in techniques or strategies among schools of family therapy and the effectiveness of the various strategies have been studied (Anderson, Atilano, Bergen, Russell, & Jurich, 1985).

A classification system consisting of 21 categories representing the clinical techniques of the structural, strategic, and behavioral schools of therapy was constructed. The correlation of techniques used and successful completion versus premature termination of treatment was computed. Successful completion of treatment was found to be associated with clinicians' use of the following techniques: firming up appropriate boundaries, conflict escalation, establishing individual boundaries, and advice giving. Early termination was associated with clinician use of problem-solving training and probing. Furthermore, analysis of techniques used in the first session of treatment indicated that clinician behaviors that were affectively intense and "shook up" the family's current interactions were predictive of continuance. Clinician behaviors in the first session that significantly predicted continuance included escalating conflict, advice giving, paradoxical interventions, conflict diffusing, homework prescriptions, and restructuring dysfunctional subsystem boundaries.

The importance of this study lies in its operationalization and common definition of techniques or strategies common to several family therapy approaches, which were then used to evaluate outcome. It demonstrated that complex theoretical definitions could be operationally defined and that the effects of various clinician skills or techniques could be empirically evaluated. Studies of this nature provide information about the clinical process that not only benefits clients but also improves theoretical conceptualizations about the nature of practice.

Feminist Practice

Feminist philosophy and analysis have recently been applied to social work practice. Frequently, however, the ways in which feminist practice differs from more traditional approaches have not been specified. Russell (1984) analyzed feminist practice into five main counseling skills to determine whether a training course in these skills could modify practitioners' behavior and attitudes.

Using Ivey's (1971) microcounseling paradigm by which complex clinical processes are divided into observable units, Russell identified five central feminist counseling skills. These skills were defined as positive evaluation of women, social analysis, encouragement of total development, self-disclosure, and behavioral feedback. Results of the skill training study indicated that skills of social analysis and androgyny encouragement were significantly increased through training, and attitudes toward women changed in the positive direction among clinical trainees.

The importance of this study again relates primarily to the definition of skills or techniques of the feminist approach. The effectiveness of these techniques in producing client change, however, was not assessed.

SUMMARY

Studying the clinical process has proved difficult in both psychotherapy and in social work. Complex interactions between clients and clinicians tend to be elusive and are not easily captured in concrete research paradigms. However, the efforts of social work researchers have provided beginning insight into and understanding of the clinical process.

The majority of social work studies in this area have followed conventional, rigorous research methods. Reid (1987) suggested that increased inquiry would result if practitioners and researchers understood that all inquiry does not have to uphold rigorous experimental standards. It can be viewed as exploratory and descriptive. Rough and dirty studies can be considered valid in the sense that they suggest which clinical processes and/or clinician behaviors are likely to be beneficial and therefore worthy of further study.

Empirical study of the various components of the clinical process has yielded considerable information that clinicians can utilize to improve their practice. Empirical data regarding structure of process can be transferred directly into modifications of clinical practice. Further knowledge regarding the ways in which practice can be modified to become more effective has been developed through clinical outcome studies.

Chapter 6

OUTCOME IN INDIVIDUAL INTERVENTION

Until recently individual interventions were not treated separately in the social work evaluation literature. Historically, social work interventions were not specified by type in evaluation studies, but rather various types of interventions were grouped together under the casework rubric. Studies of casework effectiveness, thus, in fact were investigations of various types of interventions, including individual, group, and family interventions, as well as unspecified combinations of all three. Furthermore, only limited specification of the nature of interventions was presented; descriptions ranged from informal provision of friendship to formal and intensive provision of psychotherapy. This lack of specificity led Fischer (1973) to conclude that the only commonality in definitions of casework was that it consisted of service provided by a MSW-level practitioner.

Recent studies of clinical intervention have been considerably more specific in describing the nature, type, and content of intervention. Group, couple, family, and individual interventions have all been described and studied separately, creating distinct compendia of knowledge about each. Furthermore, within each area, a variety of specific interventive approaches have been described and researched. The present review, therefore, treats individual, group, couple, and family interventions as separate types of interventions and reviews the research related to each type of intervention in a separate chapter.

Another difficulty with early studies of casework effectiveness is their lack of specificity in describing client problems. Client problems frequently were vaguely defined, for example, as "pre-delinquent behavior among acting-out adolescents," or "unspecified family problems among economically dependent populations." In addition, in early studies of casework effectiveness, clients frequently neither perceived themselves as having problems nor voluntarily sought help for them.

Recent investigations, in contrast, have tended to be problem-specific, a development that has resulted in the development of bodies of knowledge, including problem-specific journals and publications, related to specific problems. Much of this knowledge has been generated by interdisciplinary inquiry by social work researchers. Inasmuch as the scope of the present review does not permit inclusion of this problem-specific literature, it is limited to studies of more general interventions and problem-specific interventions presented in the social work journals that were reviewed. This review, therefore, cannot be considered comprehensive in terms of social work inquiry into specific problem designations. Problem-specific studies are most comprehensively presented and reviewed in journals devoted to the topic.

OUTCOME EVALUATION IN SOCIAL WORK

The types of questions asked by clinical researchers in social work have been more diverse than those posed by psychotherapy researchers, who have focused largely on outcome evaluation. Social work researchers have posed exploratory and descriptive questions in addition to explanatory or outcome questions. Social work researchers have explored and described emerging social problems as well as tested theories related to such problems, and their research has not been limited to experimental designs or formal tests of intervention outcomes. One consequence of this broader perspective has been the development of external pressure to provide more outcome evaluation studies.

These pressures have originated from both consumers and funders of social work services, who have demanded that inefficient, unprofessional, or unethical interventions be discontinued (Kutchins & Kirk, 1987). Legislation also has been implemented to regulate clinical social work standards. These standards provide benchmarks against which consumers can launch legal actions to redress perceived grievances. Funders and administrators of social work services have developed standardized financial reimbursement protocols that require clinical social workers to deliver services that are cost effective (Miller & Rehr, 1983). The result of all of these external pressures, as well as professional obligations for ethical practice, has been the recognition that accountable outcome evaluation has become a necessary, rather than an optional, aspect of clinical intervention. Increasingly, social workers have realized that, at least in part, the continued development, and perhaps even the existence, of clinical social work practice depend on providing empirical data regarding effectiveness and efficiency of interventions. Although such concerns were not as prevalent in the past as they are today, they also served to instigate early social work studies.

HISTORICAL OVERVIEW

Early reviews of social work outcome studies were primarily aimed at developing "box scores," enumerating and comparing the number of studies with positive results to those with negative results. The nature of the studies reviewed frequently did not allow for critical evaluation or assessment of the nature of intervention provided. In some studies, the extent to which the prescribed intervention had been provided was unclear. Since detailed descriptions of interventions often were not provided, it was difficult to draw inferences regarding helpful or harmful aspects of clinical practice.

Furthermore because client problems were defined diffusely and globally, outcome measures tended to be similarly global and not sensitive to smaller individual changes. In addition, the interventions studied, which usually had a psychological focus, were only marginally linked to the social problems of the clients. While these shortcomings were recognized by individual researchers, who frequently presented their results tentatively and with many cautions, they were not considered at length by reviewers, who instead tabulated box scores that led to the frequently reiterated conclusion that casework was ineffective.

In many ways, the early reviews of social work outcome were influenced by Eysenck's (1952) review of psychotherapy, which purported to demonstrate that psychotherapy provided no benefits over spontaneous remission rates. The ensuing debate in the psychotherapy literature about the nature of psychotherapy, the definition of spontaneous remission, and the design of psychotherapy evaluations was paralleled in the social work literature. In social work, as in psychology, this debate resulted in clarification of the nature and purpose of clinical intervention and to improvements in the design of studies, including more specific delineation of outcome. As a result, reviews of social work effectiveness research, like psychotherapy effectiveness research, have moved from considerable pessimism, regarding all interventions as ineffective, to cautious optimism about the effectiveness of specific interventions (Lambert, Shapiro, & Bergin, 1986; Reid & Hanrahan, 1982).

The shift in the tone of social work effectiveness reviews occurred between reviews of studies completed before 1973 and those completed after 1973. Both the nature of the evaluation studies included in the reviews and the conclusions reached by the reviewers changed. The present review, therefore, considers these two periods separately.

Outcome Studies Before 1973

In the 1950s and 1960s several large-scale experimental studies of social work interventions cast doubt on the effectiveness of casework practice. One of the earliest summaries of these findings was provided by Grey and Dermody's (1972) review of six studies, three related to juvenile delinquency and three related to problems of economically dependent families. This review noted that positive benefits were found for casework services over no intervention in three studies but that no significant difference was found in the remaining three studies. In all six cases, however, the interventions studied were neither well defined nor limited to individual interventions. Instead the interventions consisted of various combinations of loosely defined, multifaceted types of interventions that varied in duration and intensity. Furthermore, interventions were provided indiscriminately to both voluntary and involuntary client groups.

In discussing these six studies, Grey and Dermody (1972) noted what they referred to as the gap between philosophy and practice. In particular they discussed the limitations of providing interventions designed for voluntary, motivated, psychologically distressed clients to involuntary clients suffering primarily from social and/or economic deficits. The gap, in short, was between psychologically oriented interventions and a socially and economically deprived clientele.

Segal (1972) reviewed the same six studies of dependent families and delinquent children along with a number of psychotherapy studies. On the basis of his review, Segal concluded that social work and psychotherapy interventions overall had been ineffective. He suggested that, in both social work and in psychotherapy, there was a need to delineate specific intervention techniques, as well as to specify realistic intervention-linked goals for specific problems and/or populations.

Given the lack of definition of social work intervention techniques and the lack of specific intervention-linked goals, early social work researchers faced a number of problems. These were summarized by Mullen, Chazin, and Feldstein (1972):

> Ideally the helping professions would have explicated what might be called a series of "problem-intervention-outcome" typologies that would specify in unambiguous terms the types of problems each attempts to prevent or ameliorate, the specific nature of the interventions used for each of the problems, and the expected effects of each of the interventions. Such typologies would serve as a guide to the evaluator by pointing clearly to the nature of the particular problem goal to be assessed. Needless to say, such an idealized state is far from realized. (p. 317)

As a result, the authors claimed, the evaluative criteria utilized in research was imprecise and arbitrary. Furthermore, studies were plagued by a number of methodological difficulties, including limited knowledge of target populations, irregular implementation of interventions, poor problem definition, and use of control groups that were really contrast groups. Rather than drawing conclusions about casework effectiveness based on ill-conceived comparisons, Mullen, Chazin, and Feldstein (1972) suggested another approach might be more appropriate:

> One might conclude, if one were not convinced of it already, that persons who need primarily money, jobs and housing, may be served quite well by workers who are accustomed to dealing with the provision of tangible services and that work on problems of social and emotional adjustment may not be needed or wanted until survival needs have been met . . . service alone, in the absence of an opportunity structure, cannot solve problems of poverty and delinquency. (pp. 430-431)

The casework effectiveness debate was brought into prominence in the social work literature by Joel Fischer. Fischer's (1973) review focused on 11 studies that were considered to meet the criteria of adequate control and professional service. The studies reviewed, which were basically the same studies used in earlier reviews, focused on delinquency prevention and family problem resolution for financially dependent families, although studies of services to the institutionalized elderly and female parolees were also included. The institutionalized elderly receiving social work services, in the studies reviewed by Fischer (Bleckner, Bloom & Nielson, 1971; Killian, 1970), were found to have higher mortality rates than those not receiving such services. However, a number of subsequent re-analyses of these data failed to find negative effects of social work intervention (Berger & Piliavin, 1976; Dunkle, Poulschock, Silverstone, & Deimling, 1983; Fischer & Hudson, 1976).

Of all the studies included in the Fischer's review, the study of casework with female probationers (Webb & Riley, 1970) was the one in which individual services were most clearly and regularly provided. Significant pre- and post-intervention differences were found on a variety of psychological indicators, but Fischer discounted them in his review because the study lacked comparative group analyses. Instead Fischer emphasized the negative findings in 9 of the 11 studies he reviewed.

Fischer's (1976) review added six additional studies to those included in his earlier review, including studies of psychoanalytic services to children, further studies of services to predelinquents, and studies of services to maritally distressed women. The additional studies on children and adolescents, which again reported predominantly negative findings, were similar to those in the earlier review in that they suffered from lack of attention to environmental influences. The studies on married women added a new dimension to the review, providing a significantly different population of study. The positive results of counseling maritally distressed women in one study (Most, 1964), however, were again discounted by Fischer because the study had not used appropriate statistical tests. Commenting on Fischer's review, Werner (1976) observed that the studies on marital conflict were the only studies in which client problems were not massively influenced by socio-economic environments or chronic physical conditions. Furthermore they were the only studies that described the provision of a regime of regular interventions of a nonpsychoanalytic orientation. The positive findings of these studies, Werner suggested, should not be totally discounted, in spite of the lack of statistical tests.

Fischer (1978) extended his review of social work evaluation studies to include effectiveness research in psychotherapy, counseling, corrections, psychiatric hospitalization, and education. Given the lack of significant and consistent positive research findings, he concluded that there was little or no empirical evidence to validate any of these professional efforts. As in earlier reviews, professional practice, rather than research design, was considered to be limited and imperfect.

In contrast to the conclusions reached by other reviewers, Alexander and Simon (1973) suggested that evaluative methods rather than practice methods were inadequate. The possibility was raised that if evaluative methods had been more sensitive, if studies had been able to isolate interventive effects from environmental effects, conclusions might have been different.

The last of the pre-1973 research reviews, which included and extended previously cited studies, was presented by Wood (1978). Her review consisted of 22 studies and, in contrast to earlier reviews that equated casework with MSW-level service, included studies of casework services provided by non-MSWs. It also included studies described as quasi-experimental; earlier reviews had included only rigorous experimental designs. Wood further reviewed studies by types of populations and types of services, and attempted to draw useful practice inferences from results. For example, she pointed out that group programs that combined delinquent and impressionable "pre-delinquent" children may have fostered identification and association with delinquent behaviors and attitudes by predelinquents, resulting in increased rather than decreased delinquency rates. She suggested that social workers need to take more care in considering group composition and intra-group influences. Wood also commented on the need for environmental interventions for deprived populations.

In spite of this repeated message regarding the need for social workers to attend to environmental interventions, little change from the predominantly intrapsychic interventions has been noted. Grinnell and Kyle (1975), surveying a sample of caseworkers, found that environmental interventions ranked 12th out of a total of 18 possible interventions and composed only 3% of total interventions.

However, the message regarding the necessity for increased specificity of interventions and matching of outcome indicators with the nature of interventions appeared to have more direct results. Studies of casework effectiveness completed after 1973 were markedly different from earlier studies.

Outcome Evaluation After 1973

In 1981 Fischer suggested that a quiet revolution had occurred in social work practice and that progress had been made toward a more empirically based scientific model of practice. While he provided no evidence for this claim, several subsequent reviews supported his assertions in that outcomes reported were consistently more positive.

Reid and Hanrahan (1982) reviewed 22 studies published after 1973 and noted an increase in structured interventions aimed at specific goals, with subsequently more positive outcomes. Eight of the studies reviewed dealt with adult adjustment problems, two investigated additive effects of social work intervention with drug treatment for psychiatric patients, and four involved structured marital interventions. Except for treatment of severely disturbed psychiatric patients, positive treatment effects were reported. Reid and Hanrahan concluded that clinical interventions by social workers were largely effective, particularly when structured approaches addressed specific problems and when client-clinician congruence existed regarding motivation and expectations. Furthermore, they suggested that when clinicians provided a sharper focus to their interventions, researchers or evaluators were able to pursue more focused and relevant studies.

Reid and Hanrahan's (1982) review was criticized by Fischer (1983), who questioned the adequacy of the data analyses of several of the studies they reviewed, and by Epstein (1983) who criticized the limited selection of studies and goals in studies reviewed. However, given the recommendations of earlier evaluation studies for greater specificity of both intervention and outcome measures, the criticism regarding limited focus seems inconsistent. Furthermore, using lack of appropriate statistical analyses to dismiss the findings observed is of little relevance when size of observed effects is large enough to be of practical significance. Reid and Hanrahan's cautiously optimistic observations of the progress made in both delineation of clinical interventions and appropriate evaluation methods appeared to be warranted.

Thomlison (1981, 1984) continued the positive trend of clinical reviews in considering outcome studies from psychotherapy, marital therapy, family therapy, and behavioral therapy. The rationale used for expanding the range of studies was that these interventions were frequently used by social work clinicians, and therefore the findings were of relevance to social workers. On the basis of his reviews Thomlison concluded that sufficient positive evidence had accumulated regarding effectiveness of these approaches to support their use. The suggestion was made that clinicians should concern themselves with developing the most efficient interventions, those that produced the greatest change in the least time as well as those that produced the most durable changes. Thomlison concluded that sufficient empirical data did not exist to choose between alternate interventions.

Simons (1984), in contrast, suggested that evidence regarding the relative effectiveness of different clinical interventions did exist. According to Simons, evidence supporting behavioral interventions for treatments of phobias, child management problems, and certain adult mental health problems over alternate approaches was to be found. Furthermore, in treatment of marital distress, he suggested that evidence supported conjugal over individual interventions and communication skills training over other intervention modalities. It has been recognized, however, that for the myriad problems for which social workers provide interventions, little evidence regarding effectiveness of alternate approaches exists.

Most recently, Rubin (1985) reviewed 12 social work outcome studies reported between 1978 and 1983. Rubin continued in the optimistic vein, concluding that positive effects predominated particularly in cases of structured, well-defined interventions with specific goals and logically linked procedures. Rubin also explicated the notion of providing differential treatment based on client characteristics and problems. He noted, for example, that cognitive interventions were beneficial for clients with life-change problems or negative self-evaluations, but were deleterious for severe disturbances such as chronic schizophrenia. Rubin also distinguished between case management and personal adjustment functions of social work interventions. Case management functions were considered to have positive outcomes in dealing with the seriously ill or disabled, whereas interventions for personal adjustment functions were found to be most positive for those clients with problems-in-living.

Summarizing the changes in social work practice that resulted from these effectiveness studies, Sheldon (1987) listed the following: clearer and more concrete definitions of problems, reduction of intervention goals, greater use of behavioral and contractual interventions, and greater use of monitoring devices to provide feedback for both clients and clinicians. Sheldon concluded that practice and research had progressed in tandem to provide a more optimistic picture of social work intervention.

While the general tenor of outcome reviews changed over the decade of the 1970s from negative to guardedly positive, recognition of the potential negative effects of interventions has been sustained over time. Understanding the circumstances in which negative effects occur has been deemed increasingly necessary in order to prevent their occurrence.

DETERIORATION EFFECTS OF CLINICAL INTERVENTION

Psychotherapy reviews have consistently concluded that a proportion of clients, with estimates ranging up to 10%, show negative outcomes or actual deterioration as a result of clinical intervention (Bergin & Lambert, 1978; Lambert, Shapiro, & Bergin, 1986). In outcome studies, these negative effects can cancel out positive effects, yielding a null effect of intervention. Both clinician characteristics and client characteristics have been shown to correlate with deterioration effects.

Client characteristics most frequently found to be associated with deterioration include severity of disturbance and particular diagnoses such as schizophrenia and borderline personality. The risk of deterioration has been found to be exacerbated when coupled with clinical interventions aimed at breaking down, challenging, or undermining habitual coping strategies of defenses.

Clinician behaviors most frequently found to correlate with client deterioration have included the use of aggressive tactics that failed to account for client fragility, tendencies to over-identify or be caught up in clients' depression and helplessness, and failure to structure or focus the interventive process (Lambert, Shapiro, & Bergin, 1986).

In social work research deterioration effects have been observed and discussed by several reviewers. Wood (1978) noted the propensity for group programs for pre-delinquent children to foster delinquent behavior through association and identification with older, more established delinquents. Fischer (1978), who discussed deterioration effects extensively, urged clinicians to rid themselves of the "rescue fantasy," the idea that they could help all clients. Rubin (1985), more specifically, discussed the inappropriateness of psychodynamic interventions for chronically mentally ill or disabled clients, and echoed psychotherapy reviewers in promoting case-management interventions for these populations.

In social work research, much of the positive evidence regarding specific treatment for specific populations or problems has been generated by proponents of task-oriented and other similarly structured interventions.

STRUCTURED INTERVENTIONS

The superiority of structured behavioral approaches has been reiterated in several social work outcome reviews (Fischer, 1978; Reid & Hanrahan, 1982). Thyer and Hudson (1987) contended not only that structured interventions were more effective but also that they were more congruent than other approaches with the person-in-situation perspective of social work.

Reid and his associates generated considerable evidence to support structured approaches in developing the task-centered approach. Beginning with the investigation of differences between short- and long-term interventions (Reid & Shyne, 1969), moving to the development of a short-term structured model of intervention (Reid & Epstein, 1972), and generalizing the model to a number of different population groups and settings (Goldberg, Gibbons, & Sinclair, 1985; Reid & Epstein, 1977), their investigations have consistently provided support for short-term, structured interventions. While clarity of problem definition, goal setting, and evaluation have been important aspects of this approach, its most significant contribution has been the analysis and description of interventions. Task-oriented intervention has been defined as a composite of planning tasks, establishing incentives and rationale, generating alternatives, reaching agreement, analyzing obstacles, and structuring implementation to include simulations and guided practice (Reid, 1978).

Evaluation of the task-centered approach began with testing the effectiveness of the task-implementation sequence (TIS) in single sessions (Reid, 1975). The TIS consisted of enhancing commitment, planning task implementation, analyzing obstacles, modeling, rehearsal, guided practice, and summarizing. This sequence was randomly applied to an experimental group in the fourth interview, while an unstructured problem discussion was held in the control group. Significantly superior task attainment was found in the experimental group, particularly in relation to unique, as opposed to repetitive, tasks. In a subsequent study, Reid (1978) compared the effectiveness of the task-centered approach with equivalent supportive treatment provided over the first six weeks of interventions and found significantly better results for task-centered interventions. A cross-over design was then implemented with the previously supported clients receiving task-centered interventions as well. Again significant gains over previous task achievement rates were observed.

Reid and Epstein (1977) presented a series of descriptive studies of the task-centered approach in various settings. Successful implementation was reported in settings as diverse as public welfare agencies, schools, hospitals, correctional agencies, industrial settings, and child guidance and family service agencies. However, the evaluations reported were limited to assessment of goal attainment and lacked comparison groups or controls.

A series of quasi-experimental studies investigated task-centered approaches in three different British settings: a general social service department, a probation service, and a suicide prevention service (Goldberg, Gibbons, & Sinclair, 1985). The most rigorous of these studies was the suicide prevention project where clients were assigned either to a regular service, which consisted primarily of assessment and referral to a general practitioner or psychiatrist, or to an experimental task-centered follow-up by social workers. Client satisfaction measured at 4- and 18-month follow-up clearly indicated client preference for the task-centered approach. Other outcome indicators were mixed. Repeated suicide attempts were not significantly decreased by the task-centered approach, but significant improvement was noted in social and interpersonal problems, mood, and subsequent use of psychiatric services. Improvement was noted primarily in moderate- and low-risk clients, particularly younger women with relationship problems. High-risk clients, those with a history of previous suicide attempts or diagnoses or sociopathy or alcoholism, had equivalent outcomes regardless of intervention type (Gibbons, Bow, & Butler, 1985; Gibbons, Bow, Butler, & Powell, 1979).

The study of probation services compared the outcome of clients who received task-centered interventions with aggregate follow-up data of other probationers. A somewhat lower reconviction rate was found for clients in the task-centered project (Goldberg, Stanley, & Kenrich, 1985). Client satisfaction was reported to be high among the task-centered group. Tasks considered particularly appropriate with this population were interpersonal difficulties and problems in role performance, primarily employment.

The study of task-centered approaches in a public social service department (Sinclair & Walker, 1985) indicated most clearly the limitations of this approach. Only one-third of the cases ultimately received this intervention. The difficulties encountered were largely ascribed to characteristics of the client group, who were described as dependent because of age or physical condition. Furthermore, the nature of service was frequently prescribed by an agency other than clients themselves, including mandated services of a protective or ameliorative nature. In such cases, the task-centered approach was found to be inappropriate.

In general, the task-centered approach has been considered of limited utility with the minority of clients who cause the greatest difficulties for themselves and for others. Clients with the most serious employment, criminal, or psychological problems were the least helped. In addition, application was limited to instances in which worker and client agreed on problems, actions, and the likelihood of successful problem resolution. It was suggested that the task-centered approach was best suited to the middle range of clients, those whose problems were neither pervasive nor deep-seated.

Limitations of the task-centered approach were also reviewed by Kanter (1983), who noted that the approach originally had been contraindicated for neurotics, psychotics, character disorders, substance abusers, or individuals motivated by existential concerns or grieving personal losses. He also emphasized that the approach was unlikely to be successful with the more severely disturbed, including clients with diagnoses of character-disorder, borderline personality, or schizophrenia.

O'Connor and Reid (1986) discussed findings of dissatisfaction with brief treatment by a portion of clients studied. They noted that these clients tended to be women who were attempting to function more independently despite chronic low self-esteem. The extent to which the principles of brief interventions could be adapted to this group remained undetermined.

Several reviews of interventions with the mentally ill have emphasized the benefits of structured behavioral interventions (Rubin, 1984; Rubin, 1985; Wilner, Freeman, Surber, & Goldstein, 1985; Wong, Woolsey, & Gallegos, 1987). Behavioral interventions that provided rewards for the gradual acquisition of positive behaviors were typically found to result in beneficial outcomes. However, the results did not generalize to mentally ill clients who also had alcohol or drug abuse problems or to clients in active psychotic states.

Berlin (1980, 1985) reported a series of investigations of cognitive-behavioral interventions designed to decrease self-criticism in women. While marked decreases in levels of self-criticism were observed, the extent to which these differed from those found for attention-placebo controls and the extent to which the decreases could be maintained over time were questions only partially answered in these studies.

Reviews of social work studies in health care settings have revealed that interventions frequently involved psychoeducational or skill training approaches (Peterson & Anderson, 1984). Subramanian and Rose (1985, 1988), for example, evaluated the use of cognitive-behavioral approaches in pain management. Significant decreases in psychosocial dysfunctioning and negative mood were observed both at post-treatment and at two-year follow-up in these studies. Similar positive findings were reported in several other studies, but most of these lacked adequate control or comparison groups.

In summary, behavioral approaches, such as the task-centered approach, have been extensively developed and investigated in the social work literature. The benefits of these approaches have been demonstrated in a variety of settings. However, their application has been limited largely to problems of an interpersonal or role performance nature. Problems of a more serious or deep-seated nature and lack of client-clinician concordance regarding problems and/or resolution have been found to contraindicate use of the task-centered approach. Most studies of the task-centered approach have been based on quasi-experimental research designs. This type of design has been adopted by many social work researchers and warrants further consideration.

SINGLE CASE EVALUATION

Incorporation of single case evaluation (SCE), or quasi-experimental, designs into social work research has been a significant change over the past two decades. Bloom (1983) described the historical origins of this methodology as arising from early promotion of systematic decision-making, rigorous observation, and outcome evaluation by pioneer social workers such as Mary Richmond and Richard Cabot. Bloom suggested that these were precursors of more recent prescriptions for objective intervention and outcome measurement by behaviorally oriented social workers. Explication and promotion of single subject design as a vehicle for social work practitioners to evaluate their own practice flourished in the 1970s (Bloom & Block, 1977; Howe, 1974; Hudson, 1977; Jayaratne, 1977; Jayaratne & Levy, 1979; Levy & Olson, 1979). The benefits of single case procedures in monitoring progress with particular types of interventions, such as marital and family interventions, were demonstrated (Bloom, Butch & Walker, 1979; Mutschler, 1979; Witkin & Harrison, 1979).

Despite this surge of positive interest in SCE designs as a method of integrating research and practice, several limitations were noted. Thomas (1978) discussed conflicts between research requirements, such as fixed intervention phases, predetermined and limited goals, and standardized interventive methods, and practice requirements, such as flexibility and responsiveness to client needs. Thomas suggested that these conflicts could prohibit full-scale implementation of SCE designs in clinical practice or necessitate substantial design modification. Thomas concluded that practical constraints such as time limits, premature termination, and change of client focus and/or life events could result in limited integration of research and practice. Gambrill and Barth (1980), however, countered, saying that this view was overly pessimistic, and that as accountability in practice increased in importance, the goals and purposes of research and practice would increasingly coalesce. Furthermore, they suggested that limitations in research design necessitated by practice requirements could be overcome through replication of studies and the accumulation of data over time.

Replication of single case studies has been considered essential to allow generalization of findings (Jayaratne & Daniels, 1981; Kazdin, 1979). Guidelines for clinical replications and the means by which clinical replication can test theory as well as generate new clinical practices have been discussed (Barlow, Hayes, & Nelson, 1984; Hersen & Barlow, 1976). Opinion remains divided, however, regarding the extent to which SCE studies can test theory. Bloom and Fischer (1982), for example, argued that negative findings related to practice theory evidenced in a single case study can be considered sufficient evidence for the need to modify theory, while Rubin and Babbie (1989) suggested that SCE studies can best be regarded as pilots for group designs.

The benefits of SCE designs have extended beyond simple utility of clinical self-monitoring and practice evaluation. Nugent (1987) discussed the value of considering SCE data in addition to group data, pointing out that paying attention to the latter alone can obscure valuable information about within group, or individual, differences. SCE data, in contrast, provide this information very clearly. Nuehring and Pascone (1986) discussed the utility of SCE designs in peer reviews as part of quality assurance programs. Campbell (1988) demonstrated that clients respond favorably to SCE implementation, preferring systematic monitoring procedures over use of clinician judgment of progress alone. Recognizing the need for such monitoring devices, social work researchers have directed considerable effort to issues of clinical measurement.

MEASUREMENT OF CLINICAL OUTCOME

Rapid Assessment Instruments

One of the consequences of promoting research-practice integration has been the necessity of developing sensitive, valid, and reliable measures of client change that can be used briefly and repeatedly in clinical settings. Two types of measures have emerged: standardized measures with corresponding norms and cut-off points, and unstandardized or individualized scale that conform to a designated format.

Standardized clinical measures of this nature have been termed Rapid Assessment Instruments (RAIs), and their utility in assessing client change has been documented (Levitt & Reid, 1982; Toseland & Reid, 1985). The development of a package of measures specifically developed for social work interventions by Hudson (1982) has further promoted the use of such measures, as has the compendium of clinical measures compiled by Corcoran and Fischer (1987).

Individualized measures for monitoring change have largely been based on Kiresuk and Sherman's (1968) Goal Attainment Scaling (GAS) model. Although the model was originally developed for evaluating program effectiveness and has been used for that purpose by social workers in health settings (Rock, 1987; Spano, Kiresuk, & Lund, 1978), its use in both monitoring clinical practice and providing feedback for clinical decision-making also has been advocated and demonstrated (Justice & Justice, 1976). A variation of this measure, developed in the context of social work research, is the Individual Problem Rating (IPR) (Gillespie & Seaberg, 1977; Orme, Gillespie, & Fortune, 1983; Seaberg, 1981). Another variation, initially developed by Weed (1969) for medical settings, is the Problem Oriented Record (POR), which has spawned a number of variations and permutations (Beinecke, 1984). In addition, various types of self-monitoring and self-rating techniques used in both research and clinical practice were reviewed by Kopp (1988).

Client Satisfaction Measures

Measures of client satisfaction have increasingly been included as indicators of intervention outcome as consumers have demanded a voice in service delivery (Rehr, 1983). The consumer's voice has come to be regarded as a necessary component of quality assurance (Garber, Brenner, & Litwin, 1986), and the uniqueness and validity of the consumer's perspective has been recognized (Sainsbury, 1987). Measures of consumer satisfaction have ranged from relatively unsophisticated one- or two-item surveys regarding service satisfaction (Blumberg, Ely, & Kerbeshian, 1975) to in-depth, focused interviews that probe client perceptions of treatment outcomes (Magura, 1982; Maluccio, 1979), to multi-item ratings of a range of social work functions (Garber, Brenner, & Litwin, 1986; Rubenstein & Bloch, 1978). Involvement of consumers in the development, pretesting, and analysis of consumer measures was reported in an evaluative survey of psychiatric patients that resulted in several significant changes in program delivery (Selig, Reber, Phanidis, & Robertson, 1982). Based partially on these earlier investigations, several standardized measures of consumer satisfaction that can be applied across settings and types of services have been developed (Larsen, Attkisson, Hargreaves, & Nguyen, 1979; Reid & Gundlach, 1983).

In general consumer surveys have reported high satisfaction levels, particularly when global ratings were used, leading some researchers to coin these responses as "grateful testimonials" (Ware, Snyder, Wright, & Davies, 1983). To avoid this effect, the use of multidimensional scales that evaluate various aspects of intervention or service has been recommended (Locker & Dunt, 1978). However, some of the difficulties inherent in the use of multi-dimensional scales were demonstrated by Reid and Gundlach (1983), who found that when clients were asked to evaluate social workers they stated that they did not know whether services were adequately defined or whether their social workers knew what they were doing. It is clear, nevertheless, that methods of client involvement, such as those demonstrated by Selig and colleagues (1982), have promise for the development and extension of measures of intervention outcome that are not only valid but also useful in modifying interventions.

SUMMARY

Social work effectiveness studies have come a long way from the early assessments of global goals in nonspecified interventions with economically and socially deprived populations to the current evaluations of specific interventions with specific populations using standardized measures. These changes have resulted in more positive evaluations of outcome as well as in refinements in clinical interventions. Whether the current, more selective, evaluations adequately represent the totality of social work intervention, however, is still open to debate.

It has been suggested that social problems today are proliferating and changing at a considerably higher rate than solutions can be provided, and at a much greater rate and extent than the ability of researchers to investigate them (Jenkins, 1987). High-priority social problems, such as AIDS, homelessness, violence, and substance abuse, are only beginning to be studied. It is incumbent on the profession not only to promote such study but also to demonstrate through investigation the particular benefits that social work intervention can provide.

Chapter 7

OUTCOME IN GROUP INTERVENTION

Reviews of group psychotherapy research provide a useful starting point for the review of social group work intervention. In their review of group psychotherapy research, Kaul and Bednar (1986) pointed out that professional and ethical considerations require placing primary importance on outcome research. They observed that, because systems of psychological help-giving have been notorious for producing fads, movements of near missionary zeal, and unsubstantiated claims, professionals need to continually evaluate new and emerging approaches. Lang (1979) echoed this concern in relation to social work, stating that because social work incorporates theoretical material from other social and behavioral sciences it may be unduly susceptible to such transitory fads. Furthermore, social work has a less well-developed empirical base against which to evaluate effectiveness claims.

Group interventions, in particular, appear to have been susceptible to trends and fads, perhaps because social interaction in groups is experienced by many individuals as intrinsically satisfying and groups of any nature therefore have some appeal. However, in order to validate the clinical or therapeutic use of group interventions, some benefit besides satisfaction with social intercourse must be demonstrated. Unfortunately, in the social work literature there is not a great deal of evidence that such benefits exist. Studies of group intervention in social work, while including outcome evaluation, have also focused on other dimensions of group process. A number of studies have attempted to clarify the nature of group intervention in social work in order to differentiate between social group work and therapeutic or clinical group approaches. A number of other studies have investigated the nature of group process, and some studies have commented on the deterioration effects observed as a result of group intervention. The question of most importance, the benefit of group intervention, has received somewhat less attention than it has warranted.

STATUS OF RESEARCH IN GROUP WORK

Concern about the dearth of empirical validation of social group work intervention has been expressed in several reviews of group work literature. Feldman's (1987) review of a decade of literature indicated that only 10% of the articles on social group work could be classified as research. Not only were research articles few in number, but they were also plagued by methodological weaknesses, such as small numbers of subjects, lack of control groups or extended baselines, and lack of statistical analyses. Furthermore, when Feldman compared the results of his 1987 survey with Silverman's 1966 survey, he found an increase of only 6% in the number of research articles on group work over the intervening two decades. Furthermore, this slight increment was the most dramatic change that had occurred during this interval.

In a somewhat overlapping review of 340 group work papers, Rothman and Fike (1988), using a broader definition of research that included any mention of standardized measures or counting procedures, found 15% of the articles devoted to research. However, they noted that in the most recent years of their survey the rate of research activity was decreasing. Rather optimistically, they suggested that revised CSWE accreditation standards requiring increased research focus could be expected to reverse this trend. Whether these expectations were realistic has yet to be determined.

DEFINITION OF GROUP INTERVENTION

Group intervention has been variously defined, with much of the variability in definition reflecting different emphases placed on individual versus group processes and outcomes. Bednar and Kaul (1978), in their review of the group psychotherapy literature, took the position that group intervention consisted of more than the application of therapeutic regimes to aggregates of individuals. Their definition of group psychotherapy included the development of a social microcosm, provision of social learning based on feedback and consensual validation, and involvement of group participants in both helper and helpee roles.

In the social work literature, the definition of group intervention has been further complicated by the controversy regarding the relationship of therapeutic or clinical group interventions and social group work. Lang (1979) reviewed the differences between therapeutic work with groups and social work with groups and concluded that clinical group interventions were a separate and distinct entity, not related to social group work. Lang defined social group work as a social rather than psychological form of helping, as having goals of autonomous group development with shared group goals, as fostering naturalistic interaction with moderated worker direction, and as existing in its own right without necessarily identifying or articulating problems. Therapeutic groups, in contrast, were defined as problem focused, worker directed, and specifically aimed at resolving individual problems through the medium of group process. Lang's position, however, did not correspond to prevailing group work practice in the field.

The alternate view, that social work with groups encompasses a variety of approaches, including psychological and social influence models, has been more widely accepted and is more in accord with prevailing practice. Home and Darveau-Fournier (1982) surveyed 60 Quebec social workers regarding their use of groups and, on the basis of their results, developed a three-category system of group intervention. Social workers reported using three primary group approaches: personal change groups, developmental groups, and social change groups. They reported using the three approaches with approximately equivalent frequencies, and the majority described their role in these groups as a therapist or facilitator. In a subsequent replication of this survey with 152 Montreal social workers (Paquet-Deehy, Hopmeyer, Home, & Kislowicz, 1985), the distribution of approaches used was skewed in the direction of personal change or therapeutic groups, followed by developmental or psychoeducational groups, with social change groups used in only 7% of social worker groups.

Using a similar but differently labeled tripartite classification system, consisting of the treatment approach, the interactive or mediating approach, and traditional social group work, Cowger (1980) surveyed 192 social group work educators regarding their preferred approach to group work. Thirty-two percent chose the treatment model, 32% chose the interactive model, and 14% chose the traditional social group work model. The remaining 21% chose a variety of other approaches. Analyzing these results in terms of the age and experience of the educators revealed that the clinical or treatment model was preferred by younger, less experienced, and more recently graduated educators. The traditional social group work model was not only infrequently referred to, but also was suggested to be in decline because it was predominantly used by older educators and had not been adopted by younger ones. Cowger suggested that its decline may be due to the lack of development of social group work theory and the model's lack of amenability to effectiveness evaluation.

The traditional group work model, furthermore, has not received strong support even in past decades, as demonstrated by Levinson's (1973) review of social work literature that dated back to 1955. The results of this review indicated very clearly that social workers utilized groups primarily for treatment of individual problems.

The consistent finding among these surveys, therefore, has been that groups are utilized by social workers primarily for treatment or therapeutic goals. Whether groups led by social workers vary in any significant way from groups led by other psychotherapists has not been determined. On the assumption that they do not, the group psychotherapy literature offers some directions for both practice and research in this area.

EVALUATION OF GROUP PSYCHOTHERAPY

Bednar and Kaul (1978); Kaul and Bednar, (1986) reviewed group psychotherapy literature, selecting studies that used experimental designs with random assignment and control or matched alternate treatment groups. Twenty-eight studies were reported in their 1978 review, with an additional 16 added in their 1986 review. In both reviews the majority of studies reported significant differences between group-treated clients and non-treated control subjects on a variety of measures, including self-ratings of self-actualization, self-liking, and other self-evaluation measures. The 1978 review, which was based largely on studies of college students, reported a substantially greater proportion of positive results than the 1986 review, which consisted primarily of studies of psychologically distressed client populations.

Kaul and Bednar (1986) noted that, although a number of studies found that group interventions produce positive results, there had been little advancement in understanding causal factors in group intervention. They attributed this to the lack of research addressing the interactions of individual, process, and outcome variables. In noting that the parameters of group interventions that are causally related to outcome remain largely unknown, Kaul and Bednar suggested that this places practitioners in the "scientifically awkward position" of maintaining that there are regularities in interventive effects without being able to specify the causes or correlates of these effects. In such circumstances, they added, it is possible for superstitions and misattributions of cause-and-effect to flourish.

EVALUATION OF SOCIAL WORK GROUPS

Reviews of pre-1973 social group work studies concluded that group interventions more frequently had negative than positive effects. The early reviews by Fischer (1973, 1976) and Wood (1978) described several studies in which group interventions were coupled with individual interventions and/or family interventions in work with pre-delinquent adolescents. These studies found no positive benefits to group participants in terms of preventing subsequent antisocial behavior and, in some instances, found that the likelihood of such behavior was increased through group participation, presumably due to the influence of older, more delinquent adolescents on younger, impressionable children.

Reviews of post-1973 group work interventions, in contrast, have presented primarily positive results for the effects of group interventions. Reid and Hanrahan's (1982) review described six studies of group intervention with positive outcomes. The interventions described in these studies used primarily behavioral group methods, and the outcomes reported were typically positive. Evaluation of group outcome revealed significantly greater post-treatment gains on behaviors rated for role-play group participants over discussion group controls. Rubin's (1985) review added three more group intervention studies to the review. Again group interventions were specifically described and the interventions were aimed at specific problems among specified populations. Positive results were found for stress management training groups for women on social assistance, information provision groups for parents of ill children, and mutual aid in a support group for the elderly.

As in individual interventions, both practice and research in group interventions has moved from ill-defined, nonspecific interventions and evaluations to more focused interventions and more specific evaluations. Given this increase in focusing, however, replication and extension of studies becomes even more necessary. As in individual intervention studies, replications of group intervention studies are virtually nonexistent. Studies comparing the effectiveness of different group approaches, however, have been reported.

Effectiveness of Different Group Approaches

Behavior Change Versus Mutual Support

The debate regarding the benefits of social group work, with its emphasis on group cohesion and autonomy, compared to therapeutic group intervention, with its emphasis on behavior change, was investigated by Toseland and associates (Toseland & Rose, 1978; Toseland, Sherman, & Bliven, 1981). These studies demonstrated the importance of considering group purpose in selecting interventions. This was graphically illustrated in two studies involving group interventions with elderly clients. The 1978 study compared behavioral group methods and social group work methods in the acquisition of assertive behaviors by 53 elderly volunteers. The behavioral group method was found to be significantly superior to social group work in skill acquisition. In the 1981 study, however, the purpose of the group was to develop a mutual support system, with the nature and structure of the group defined by participants. Again, the purpose of the study was to compare behavioral group methods and social group work. This experiment, however, was modified after clients rebelled against the behavioral group methods, finding them too pedantic, structured, and inappropriate for their needs. The authors concluded that when the group purpose was remediation of individual psychological distress or deficit benefits were best derived from group approaches that were behaviorally or cognitively structured. When the aim of the group was mutual support, the more egalitarian, less structured, process-oriented social group work approach was the preferred method. The authors also suggested that in some group programs, such as those in community centers for the elderly, participants anticipate deriving pleasure and satisfaction, rather than personal change, from group participation. Social group work methods, they suggested, are more congruent with such goals.

Structured goal-oriented group interventions, however, have been found to be effective with a number of specific problems. Smoking cessation was investigated in two studies, both of which found group interventions to be more effective than no treatment (Schinke, 1979; Toseland, Kohut, & Kemp, 1983). The group interventions in both instances, while goal-specific, were multifaceted, including educational, tension-reduction, psychodynamic, and behavioral contracting techniques. The strength of the intervention was considered to lie in this multipronged focus. Social skill acquisition by sole-support mothers resulting from a group intervention was investigated by Resnick (1985). While no comparison group data were available, 73% of the group participants reported achievement of life-change goals. Furthermore, significant gains in community involvement and social support and significant decreases in emotional difficulties, psychiatric treatment, and life stress were reported over pre-group levels.

Although studies of structured group interventions have found positive results fairly consistently, the extent to which group processes are instrumental in bringing about these results has been controversial.

Group Versus Individual Goals

The relative emphases given to individual therapeutic goals and group process goals has varied considerably among studies. Lawrence and Walter (1978), for example, described a behavioral assessment and treatment model in which clinicians individually assisted clients in assessing problems and determining goals and then used the support and feedback of group interactions to promote the problem-solving process. Marshall and Mazie (1987), in contrast, described a cognitive treatment for depressed adults in which the group was used primarily to disseminate information and encourage individuals to use the prescribed methods, rather than to foster group interaction or support per se. While both approaches offered evidence of success, there is no evidence to suggest the superiority of one approach over the other. Comparative studies are needed to determine the extent to which group interactions, as opposed to individual interventions provided in group settings, foster the acquisition and/or maintenance of therapeutic gains.

In general, the results of social work group intervention studies have been in accord with group psychotherapy studies in demonstrating that behavioral approaches, which aim to induce particular skills or remedies for specific problems in a structured manner, result in positive outcomes. The additional finding that process-oriented social work groups have a function in developing systems of mutual support also has therapeutic import. However, further research is required to determine which approaches are appropriate for specific clients and client problems, as well as to determine the specific benefits of group process in the clinical enterprise.

Group Process Research

In addition to studies of group intervention outcome, several aspects of group process have been investigated. Psychotherapy studies have considered variables such as pretraining, group cohesion, self-disclosure, and feedback in the group context. Social group work studies have paralleled many of the psychotherapy investigations.

Pre-training, or education of clients about the nature of group experience, has been investigated and found to be related to positive process in group psychotherapy. Kaul and Bednar (1986) reported seven studies in which either group attendance or group behaviors improved with such training. Positive effects on outcome, however, were not consistently demonstrated. While social workers provide information to clients about the expectations of group participation, neither the systematic development of pretraining methods nor the evaluation of such methods were reported in the literature reviewed. Investigation of the benefits of pretraining would appear to be particularly pertinent for groups with high drop-out rates.

Group psychotherapy studies also have investigated the relationship of variables such as group cohesion, self-disclosure, and feedback with outcome. Kaul and Bednar (1986) concluded that, given the difficulties in comparing studies that used widely different definitions of group cohesion, conclusions about the relationship of cohesion with outcome remained equivocal. Similarly, conclusions about self-disclosure were difficult to draw due to the high variability in the social contexts of the studies. Studies related to feedback, while suggesting that positive feedback was desirable and acceptable, failed to demonstrate a consistent relationship between feedback and outcome.

Studies of group process variables have been rare in the social group work literature. Rose (1981) investigated the relationship of group cohesion, participation, and productivity in assertiveness training groups led by graduate social work students. Outcome, measured in terms of role-play performance, was found to correlate positively with participation and productivity, which was defined as completion of homework assignments. Rose noted the importance of participation, measured in terms of the ratio of members' participation to total participation, suggesting that the results demonstrated the need for group leaders to encourage member participation and to withdraw as group process became established. Rose also emphasized the importance of giving assignments and monitoring homework performance.

The process variable of self-disclosure was discussed as a predictive variables in Bostwick's (1987) review of group drop-out literature. Increased self-disclosure by clients was found to decrease clients' propensity for dropping out. Because self-disclosures are by definition participatory, these findings also supported the importance of client participation discussed above.

Group process was also monitored in a study of elderly patients in a home for the aged (Linsk, Howe, & Pinkston, 1975). By monitoring both social workers' behavior in the group and participants' responses, associations between leader behavior and group member participation were observed. Group members' participation increased as a function of the leader's questioning and attending behaviors. Encouraging behaviors were found to be important in facilitating group process.

The study of group process generally has demonstrated that group leader behaviors were important in structuring process and increasing group member participation. The importance of group leader behavior has been further emphasized in studies of group deterioration effects.

Deterioration Effects

Fischer's (1976) review of empirical studies of casework effectiveness included two studies that involved group intervention in work with pre-delinquent adolescents; both studies purported to demonstrate deterioration effects. While the reasons for deterioration were not discussed, a number of reviews have highlighted the importance of clinician behaviors. Galinsky and Schopler's (1977) review of deterioration effects in group psychotherapy studies found that clinicians who failed to define expectations regarding group process and outcome and who directed groups in a loosely structured fashion tended to have greater deterioration effects in their groups than clinicians whose instructions and communications to group members were more clear and structured. Leadership styles described as overstimulating, excessively passive, coercive, and punitive were also found to be associated with deterioration effects. This was particularly true when these leadership styles were used with group members who were psychologically unstable or highly distressed.

In reviewing deterioration effects of group intervention found in the pre-1973 social work studies, Wood (1978) commented that the loosely structured nature of groups, in conjunction with the influence of the seasoned delinquents on the pre-delinquents, may have been responsible for the negative effects observed in these studies.

The extent of deterioration effects in social work group interventions to date is largely unknown because these effects have not been monitored. As with individual intervention, the negative effects demonstrated in group psychotherapy studies are likely to be similar to those in social work group intervention. Investigation of negative, as well as positive, effects is required in future social work investigations.

Methodological Issues in Outcome Evaluation

Two methodological issues have warranted discussion in the social group work literature. The first pertains to appropriate outcome measurement, specifically, the utility of client satisfaction measures as outcome indicators. The second pertains to data analysis and the benefits and limitations of data aggregation.

Participant satisfaction measures have been used as the primary indicator of success in a number of group outcome studies. The utility of client satisfaction measures has been the subject of some debate. Fike (1980) argued against using satisfaction measures on the basis that group interaction itself can be pleasurable, and satisfaction therefore is not necessarily an indication of goal attainment or intervention effectiveness. Fike maintained that more rigorous outcome measures were needed to determine the effects of group intervention. Rose's (1981) finding that group member satisfaction was not associated with group outcome, primarily because satisfaction levels were uniformly high across groups, supported this conclusion.

Reviews of the group drop-out literature in which positive associations between satisfaction and continuance have been found lead to a different conclusion. Satisfaction with group process has been found to predict client continuance and hence to have the potential of discriminating between unsuccessful clients, or early terminators, and clients more likely to be successful, the continuers. However, at the point of termination, the satisfaction level among all participants tends to be uniformly high with little variance and hence has no predictive value in determining other outcome measures (Bostwick, 1987). Further investigation regarding the reasons for early dissatisfaction that leads to termination could provide useful clinical data.

The typical procedure used to analyze group outcome data has been to aggregate individual data and test for significant changes between pre- and post-group measures. The merits of this type of analysis, as compared to assessment of individual change of all participants, have been discussed in the social work literature (Fike, 1980; Glisson, 1987). Glisson provided an example of duplicate analyses to demonstrate that the assumptions underlying aggregate analyses were frequently erroneous. Individual differences within groups frequently have been found to be greater than differences between comparison groups. Because of such variability, reviewers have suggested that both individual and aggregate analyses be performed on group data.

SUMMARY

Clinical research in group interventions, although not abundant in social work, has nevertheless resulted in findings with important clinical implications. It has demonstrated both the variety of group approaches used by clinical social workers and the preeminence of the treatment or therapeutic group approach. The utility of the social group work approach for groups with a social support or mutual aid function has also been demonstrated. Structured group approaches have been found to produce positive findings when specific problems or deficits have been addressed. Lack of group structure and clear client expectations, as well as certain adverse leadership styles, have been associated with deterioration effects. Group process has not received much study; therefore little is known about the dynamics by which change is fostered in group situations. Further study of group process as well as outcome in clinical intervention is clearly warranted.

Chapter 8

OUTCOME IN COUPLE AND FAMILY INTERVENTIONS

Family intervention has been defined as any psychotherapeutic endeavour aimed explicitly at altering interactions between family members, or improving individual, family subsystem, or family unit functioning. Gurman, Kniskern, and Pinsof (1986), who authored this definition in their review of psychotherapy literature, stated that this definition conveyed the "complexity and variety" of the family intervention field, encompassing within it the subfields of marital or couple interventions and interventions with families of particular populations such as the mentally ill and substance abusers. Family interventions aimed at children's problems were also included in their review. The present review of clinical social work intervention has adopted the aforesaid definition, with the exception of intervention aimed at children because the focus of the present review is on adult problems and situations.

Research in the field of family intervention has progressed from broadly based studies of the general efficacy of family and marital intervention to more detailed analyses of the effects of specific types of intervention with specific client populations. Family therapy research in adult disorders has focused primarily on several major problem categories, including schizophrenia, substance abuse, affective disorders, and marital distress. In social work research, family intervention similarly has focused on problem categories. In addition, research in social work has investigated the extent and nature of use of family intervention among social workers.

USE OF FAMILY INTERVENTIONS

Family interventions or therapies have had a considerable appeal for social workers, who frequently find themselves confronting problems that involve entire families. Since family members often are involved in client problems, there is an intuitive appeal to involve them in problem solutions, despite lack of evidence or empirical documentation of the effects of such interventions (Johnson, 1986).

While a number of theories of family intervention suggest that intervention should be based on the involvement of several, if not all, family members, the institution of such recommendations has not always been practical, feasible, or even accepted as desirable. Several social work surveys have been conducted to determine the level of family involvement in clinical social work interventions.

Two surveys of social work clinicians investigated the extent to which family intervention was utilized in clinical practice. Reynolds and Cryms (1970) surveyed 61 NASW members to determine the extent to which family interviews had been conducted with the three most recent families served. Sixty-five percent of the respondents reported that they had utilized family interviews at least once. The highest rates were reported by private practitioners and clinicians with training in family therapy. Male clinicians reported somewhat higher rates of family interviews than female clinicians, but the difference was not statistically significant. The majority of clinicians reported positive attitudes toward the idea of family interviews.

Another survey (Green & Kolevzon, 1982), a decade later, was directed exclusively to family therapists. The practice of involving family members in interviews was found to be mixed, even among clinicians devoted to the family approach. The most prevalent type of clinical involvement reported was individual intervention, which accounted for 40% of total interventions. Marital or couple interventions accounted for 34% of interventions, and family interventions accounted for only 19% of the total. In spite of the predominance of individual interventions, the theory espoused by the majority of these clinicians was communication theory. Similarly, the practice goal endorsed by these clinicians was the production of understanding among family members in the context of a supportive environment.

Simply having all family members present during an interview does not guarantee that the focus of intervention will be family dynamics or family interactions. Two studies have investigated the nature of the process within family interviews. Brown (1973) studied family interview processes in terms of the focus of ascriptive statements, those providing direct feedback to clients. Brown found that, even in the context of family interviews, the vast majority of ascriptive statements were directed to individual family members; only 17% were directed to family subgroups. A similar type of analysis in relation to task-centered family interventions also revealed a predominance of individual task assignments in family-focused treatment. Reid (1987) analyzed family problem-solving sequences in clinical interventions with 47 families and found that 40% of tasks assigned were individual, an additional one-third were shared, and one-quarter were reciprocal.

The results of these studies suggest that, in spite of the appeal of family intervention, involvement of family members in interviews tends to occur relatively infrequently. Furthermore, even during the course of family intervention, the focus of intervention tends to remain largely on an individual rather than family subgroup level. It has been argued that such individual foci can be considered appropriate even in family intervention because the family is thereby appraised of the appropriateness of independent actions. However, whether similar objectives could be gained through more economical individual intervention has not been addressed. The nature of family interventions with specific types of client problems, however, has received considerable study.

Intervention with Schizophrenic Clients

Family intervention was developed in psychiatric settings, where it had been observed that schizophrenic patients who had improved frequently suffered relapses after resuming interactions with their families. One explanation for this observation, which has been offered by a number of family therapists, such as Haley (1980), is that schizophrenia is a signal of interpersonal conflict involving developmental impasses within a family. This "system purist" position, however, has failed to generate any empirical support. An alternate explanation, that schizophrenia involved a "core, biological deficit which makes a patient vulnerable to stressful stimulation from the environment," including the stress of emotionally laden family interactions, has generated considerable empirical support (Rohrbaugh, 1983, p. 30). Several studies in this area have focused on the relationship between the family's affective interaction style, or expressed emotion (EE), and the prediction of relapse among schizophrenic clients.

Platman (1983) reviewed several studies that indicated a consistent relationship between family EE and relapse rates of schizophrenics. In high EE families, relapse rates ranged from 48% to 62%, while in low EE families, rates ranged from 9% to 21%. The high EE families typically viewed the schizophrenic member negatively, interpreting withdrawal or poor personal hygiene as laziness or character weakness, whereas the low EE families exhibited warm, supportive, and disengaged behavior.

Rubin's (1984) review of social work studies in community-based care of the mentally ill also found support for the importance of family environment in preventing relapse. Specifically, for patients receiving regular medication, the most meaningful predictor of relapse was found to be the degree of disagreement and contention in the patient's home prior to treatment.

More importantly for clinical social workers, several studies have demonstrated the effectiveness of clinical intervention in modifying the behavior of high EE families. Gurman, Kniskern, and Pinsof (1986) reviewed the results of several types of family intervention that had the common goal of reducing stress on the schizophrenic member by lowering the family's "emotional temperature." Stress reduction was accomplished through psychoeducational programs that included family education about schizophrenia as an illness, use of support groups, and teaching problem-solving and crisis management strategies. In all of the studies reviewed, significant decreases in relapse rates were found when family psychoeducation was utilized as part of a follow-up program for schizophrenic patients released from hospitals.

Rubin's social work reviews (1984, 1985) echoed these conclusions, citing the work of Hogarty and associates (Anderson, Reiss, & Hogarty, 1985), who studied the effectiveness of psychoeducational approaches in working with families of schizophrenic clients. The goal was to diminish family pressure on and overstimulation of the client, increase the family's knowledge about and self-confidence in dealing with the client's illness, and improve the family's coping strategies with symptoms. Psychoeducation was found to be an effective relapse prevention approach.

Studies of family intervention with schizophrenic clients, in summary, have concluded that benefits accrue when family members' emotional involvement or expressiveness is decreased rather than increased. Psychoeducational, rather than psychodynamic approaches, have been demonstrated to be valuable. The latter have been found to produce levels of psychological distress beyond the coping abilities of emotionally vulnerable clients. The family intervention of choice with schizophrenic clients is to provide family members with information designed to promote disengagement and ability to cope with client symptoms.

Intervention with Substance Abusers

In reviewing family therapy studies in the treatment of drug and alcohol abuse, Gurman and colleagues (1986) concluded that family interventions were superior to individual clinical interventions. However, the number of studies considered was small and limited to male client populations. Janzen (1978), reviewing some of the same literature in terms of its clinical implications for social work, suggested that conclusive evidence regarding the superiority of family intervention was lacking. He did, however, cite evidence supporting spousal involvement, usually the wife, in that it was likely to decrease premature termination of treatment. The family intervention most positively discussed in Janzen's review was similar to the psychoeducational approach described above. It stressed disengagement and low emotional involvement of wives in the problems of their alcoholic husbands.

More recently, unilateral family interventions with spouses of alcoholics have been investigated and found to be effective in involving the alcoholic in treatment and/or reducing drinking levels (Thomas, Santa, Bronson, & Oyserman, 1987). The authors emphasized that the function of this type of family intervention was to use the involvement of the spouse as leverage to induce the alcoholic into treatment. The effect of this intervention on the wives, who were coached to threaten and follow through with "strong consequences" if the husbands failed to enter into treatment, was not discussed. Furthermore, the intervention in this instance was exclusively individual, in spite of family label applied to it.

Family intervention for women who suffer from alcohol or drug abuse has not been considered in the social work literature. In part this reflects the limited consideration of women generally in treatment of substance abuse. It probably also reflects the reality that husbands are less likely to remain with alcoholic wives than wives with alcoholic husbands. A considerable deficit remains, therefore, in the study of substance abuse intervention regarding the needs of women abusers, as well as the needs of women who are married or attached to male substance abusers (Corrigan, 1980; Gottlieb, 1980).

In summary, studies of family interventions for substance abusers have been limited to involvement of women as partners or mothers of male abusers. These investigations have been limited in scope, neglecting both the needs of the women in these situations and the needs of women who are themselves substance abusers. Further study that involves both sexes in an equal fashion is needed.

COUPLE INTERVENTION FOR MARITAL
CONFLICT

Clinical interventions with couples suffering from marital conflict or distress typically tend to be eclectic or based on several different schools or approaches of treatment (Gurman, Kniskern, & Pinsof, 1986; Jayaratne, 1978). In spite of this lack of adherence to particular approaches in treatment, the evaluative literature has been divided along theoretical lines: the nonbehavioral, which tends to be theoretical and descriptive, and the behavioral, which emphasizes empirical investigation.

Studies of nonbehavioral marital interventions were reviewed by Gurman and Kniskern (1978), who noted a differential rate of improvement, depending on whether one or both partners was involved in treatment. They concluded that an average improvement rate of 65% was typical of outcome studies in which both husband and wife were involved in treatment. This rate was considered equivalent to rates observed in individual intervention outcomes. In contrast, when only one spouse was involved in treatment, the rate of improvement dropped to 48%. They concluded that effective marital intervention required the involvement of both parties in treatment. A subsequent review (Gurman, Kniskern, & Pinsof, 1986), however, reached a somewhat modified conclusion, suggesting that treatment of one individual might be appropriate in instances where the problem was of an individual nature, such as depression of one partner.

Similar results regarding the benefits of conjoint marital intervention were provided in a review by Beck (1975). This review encompassed Family Services of America (FSAA) census data, doctoral dissertations regarding marital interventions, and published studies of marital interventions. Similar to the earlier review, Beck found that a 66% improvement rate was typical not only of FSAA clients but also of the clients in the other controlled studies reviewed. Furthermore, the FSAA data revealed significantly higher counselor ratings for couples treated jointly compared to those treated primarily through individual interviews. Beck concluded that, for voluntary clients seeking help primarily for relationship problems, marital counseling provided benefits on a wide range of outcome indicators.

In a critique of Beck's review, Schuerman (1975) questioned the causal inferences used to link improvement with marital intervention on the basis of FSAA data, because neither control groups nor random assignment was utilized. Furthermore, Schuerman noted, the process by which marital intervention affects dyadic relationships remains largely unknown, and further investigation of the process is necessary.

Conjoint intervention for marital problems has been compared to individual intervention in a number of social work studies whose results have differed from the foregoing. Hefner and Prochaska (1984) tested the hypothesis that individual concurrent treatment of spouses would have a greater impact on intrapersonal variables, whereas conjoint treatment would have greater effect on interpersonal variables. Their study, however, revealed no significant differences between treatments; equivalent improvement was found for both types of variables. On the basis of cost effectiveness, therefore, conjoint treatment would appear to be preferable. However, the authors warned that this advantage could be offset by the greater drop-out rates observed with conjoint treatment.

A greater drop-out rate in conjoint treatment was also observed in a study of group communication training versus conjoint marital therapy (Wells, Figurel, & McNamee, 1977). While final outcomes showed improvement for both types of interventions and no significant differences between them, the number of clients completing the conjoint treatment was significantly less than those completing the group intervention.

Behavioral marital intervention, in contrast to nonbehavioral intervention, has generated a great deal of empirical study, which has been the subject of several reviews (Bagarozzi & Giddings, 1983; Baucom & Hoffman, 1986; Gurman, Kniskern, & Pinsof, 1986). The consensus of these reviewers has been that behavioral marital intervention provides significant improvement in levels of marital distress compared to no-treatment controls. Furthermore, communication skills, which are frequently a part of such intervention packages, have been shown to be easily learned by couples with resulting increases in levels of marital adjustment and satisfaction.

Although behavioral marital intervention has been shown to produce significant improvement over no treatment, comparison with other types of marital interventions has produced mixed results. Johnson and Greenberg (1985) compared cognitive behavioral marital therapy with emotionally focused couples therapy and found the latter to be significantly superior in increasing marital adjustment scores on post-therapy testing and at eight-week follow-up. Other researchers, such as Snyder and Wills (1989) who compared behavioral and insight-oriented marital therapies, however, have found no significant differences in outcome. Several reviews of marital intervention have concluded that there is presently insufficient data to declare any one marital intervention superior to the others.

The repeated finding that various types of marital intervention produce equivalent positive gains has resulted in calls for investigations of the specific mechanisms or processes that mediate outcome. Boettcher (1977) investigated one such mechanism by studying the effects of interspousal empathy on marital satisfaction. Marital intervention resulted in significant increments in interspousal empathy, with husbands increasing substantially more than wives (because they had "further to go"). Significant correlations between gains in empathy and increased levels of marital satisfaction were observed. Boettcher concluded that interspousal empathy, particularly that of husbands, had a significant role in mediating marital satisfaction levels.

Overall, marital interventions appear to produce significant increments in levels of marital adjustment and satisfaction, but the mechanisms by which these changes are produced remains largely unexplored. Psychodynamic insight, behavior modification, and alteration of cognition all appear to produce relatively similar levels of change when studied in general populations of maritally distressed couples. Whether this indicates that some general factor in marital intervention is operating or whether differences between types of interventions have been obscured by aggregating diverse types of clients has not been determined.

As Baucom and Hoffman (1986) have pointed out, the clinical implications of this lack of difference, however, are not that any type of marital intervention is likely to be as effective as any other with specific couples and/or problems. Rather, clinical judgment is still required to make the decision about appropriate treatment. Documentation of clinical experiences is also necessary to further guide research so that relevant questions and variables can be pursued. Clinical social workers who provide marital interventions as part of their clinical practice are in an excellent position both to provide guidance to researchers and to pursue such investigations themselves.

SUMMARY

In spite of the considerable importance accorded to family systems theory in the social work literature, the accumulated evidence suggests that its impact on clinical practice has been modest. Social work clinicians, even when they identify themselves as family therapists, continue to practice primarily with individual clients, and to direct their interventions to individual goals.

Family interventions directed toward families with schizophrenic and substance-abusing members have received considerable study. Psychoeducational approaches, whereby family members are provided with information about the disorder and taught coping skills to deal with dysfunctional behavior, have consistently been found to be effective. Unfortunately, substance abuse studies have almost exclusively been limited to male clients.

Studies of interventions with couples typically have found improvement rates comparable to individual interventions, particularly when both partners were involved in counseling. Comparisons of different types of marital interventions have not indicated the superiority of any one approach.

Very little research has focused on the mechanisms by which change is produced in family or couple interventions. This is a promising area for further study and for collaboration between social work researchers and clinicians.

Chapter 9

RESEARCH ON EDUCATING
CLINICAL SOCIAL WORKERS

Social work education, as opposed to social work practice, has been the subject of comparatively extensive empirical study. Contrary to Carl Rogers' (1957) observation that psychotherapy training was subject to plenty of platitudes and rarely to research, social work education has been widely researched, albeit in a somewhat uneven manner (Sowers-Hoag & Thyer, 1985). The relative abundance of social work education research is probably due to the fact that most social work researchers find employment in educational institutions and apply their research expertise to the matter closest at hand, namely, the educational process. Although students, a pool of ready research subjects, in other disciplines are typically regarded as representative of the population at large, in social work research they tend to retain their identity as students.

The rationale for studying clinical social work education has been its eventual, and presumably direct, influence on service to clients and subsequently to client outcomes. Educational concerns have been defined as moral or ethical issues on the assumption that direct links between educational quality and quality of service exist (Task Force on Quality in Graduate Social Work Education, 1986). These links have been conceptualized as having two facets. Those of the first order, as described by Kadushin and Kelling (cited in Bloom, 1976), involve the effect of education on client outcome, through the mediation of clinician interventions. Those of the second order involve the effects of education on students. Social work research to date has almost exclusively concerned itself with the second order.

Reviews of research in social work education have not always clearly articulated the assumed connection between education and client outcome (Sowers-Hoag & Thyer, 1985), although it has been quite explicitly discussed in reviews of psychotherapy education (Matarazzo, 1978; Matarazzo & Patterson, 1986), practicum supervision (Hansen, Robins, & Grimes, 1982; Kaplan, 1983), and interpersonal skills training (Marshall, Charping, & Bell, 1979). The difficulty in testing the assumed connection between education, worker, and client outcome has been acknowledged, but little effort has been made to address it directly.

The quality of research on social work education has been highly variable. The majority of studies have been descriptive, rather than evaluative, in nature. Bloom's (1976) review of 50 studies completed prior to 1976 described them as relying primarily on judgmental evaluation or on one-shot instruments that lacked conceptual or psychometric development. A subsequent review of studies from 1975 to 1983 (Sowers-Hoag & Thyer, 1985) reported improvement in both the design of studies and the measures used, but still noted an over-reliance on relatively weak experimental designs, designs lacking in controls, and deficiencies in computation and/or reporting of comprehensive statistical analyses. Nevertheless, the degree of concurrence among studies of clinical education suggests that the composite findings of these studies have some external validity.

The present review of clinical social work education takes a broader perspective of the educational process than simply evaluation of client outcome. In the present review, research on each of the components of the educational process is considered in a manner analogous to the components of the clinical process. Studies on student and faculty characteristics are reviewed as input components; educational approaches are reviewed as process components; and studies that relate either input or process variables to learning or change are reviewed as outcome components.

STUDENTS

Characteristics of social work students have been studied in an attempt to determine which traits or characteristics predict success in clinical practice. This goal, however, has been beset by two major difficulties. The first has been the difficulty in establishing which clinician characteristics are critical to success, (see Chapter 2). The second problem has been the failure of most studies to follow students subsequent to their departure from training institutions.

Academic success typically has been used as a criteria of successful student outcome on the assumption that it mediates and/or is predictive of subsequent clinical performance. Both academic and practicum grades have been used as criteria of success. Only a few studies have attempted to investigate students' clinical performance subsequent to graduation, and those that have have used supervisor assessment or client perceptions of performance. Most studies have remained at the level of description, although some have attempted to differentiate social work students from the student population at large.

Student characteristics that have been studied have included traits subsumed under four main categories: demographics, cognitive or intellectual ability, personality or psychological traits, and values and attitudes considered relevant to social work.

Demographic Characteristics

Demographic characteristics of social work students have been considered in terms of both those that distinguish social work students from other students and those that correlate with subsequent performance. Socio-economic status (SES), age, sex, and previous social work experience have been studied.

Socio-Economic Status

Student SES has been studied mainly as an associate of attitudes or values. Merdinger (1982) compared social work, psychology, and economics students and found social work students to be of lower SES. Enoch (1988), similarly comparing Israeli social work students and other undergraduates, found that social work students reported lower socio-economic backgrounds. Both these studies and a study of values by Orten (1981) noted associations between lower SES and positive attitudes toward poverty and public dependency.

Age

Student age has been studied primarily as an intake characteristic associated with subsequent performance. Radin, Benbenishty, and Leon (1982) found that younger students, particularly those with high academic standing and graduate degrees in disciplines other than social work, were most likely to complete Ph.D.s in social work. Cunningham (1982) similarly found age and grade point average to be the only significant predictors of field performance in a study of 83 students in a bachelor of social work (BSW) program. Younger students with high academic status received the highest field performance ratings. Cunningham cited two additional doctoral dissertations both of which failed to document any positive correlation between age and performance. She concluded that the popular wisdom equating success in social work with chronological maturity needed further investigation.

Sex

The finding that females outperform males in studies of social work students has been consistently replicated. Pfouts and Henley (1977) found that female students scored significantly higher than males in field performance. Cryns (1977) found that female students were less likely than males to make attributions of personal or individual responsibility for poverty. Fortune (1984) found that female social work students were superior to males on personal problem-solving tasks. However, in spite of their superior achievements, female social work students have been found to expect lower salaries and positions than male students (Kravetz & Jones, 1982). Females' lower expectations were attributed to awareness of sex bias and discrimination in the field. Such bias, if validated, could be detrimental to the profession, given the superior achievements of women and their predominance in the field (Marsh, 1988; Merdinger, 1982).

One possible explanation for the lower performance of male students may lie in the higher levels of family disorganization reported in their families of origin. Marsh (1988) found that male social work students reported family histories of alcohol abuse and addictive/compulsive behaviors more frequently than comparable female social work students or business students of both sexes. These findings suggest that male social work students, more than female students, are likely to choose social work in order to work through or understand difficulties encountered in their own lives.

Previous Social Work Experience

The results of empirical investigation of the association of previous social work experience and subsequent academic performance have been mixed. Stein, Linn, and Furdon (1974) found that previous experience was correlated with low dogmatism scores, which in turn were associated with high academic ratings. Pfouts and Henley (1977) found previous experience was associated with high ratings in field practice. Torre (1974) found that previous experience, particularly experience supervised by social workers with master of social work (MSW) degrees, correlated with superior attainment in social work problem-solving. Cunningham (1982), however, found that previous experience was not predictive of field performance of BSW students. Bogo and Davin (1989) similarly found no correlation between work experience and either academic or practicum outcomes, and Dunlap (1979) found that two or more years of experience correlated negatively with faculty ratings of performance. Dunlap's study, however, has been criticized, on the basis of both the truncated values used in the analysis and confounding of independent and dependent variables, which both used faculty ratings (Glisson & Hudson, 1981).

Given this mixed picture of the effect of previous experience, it appears that admissions requirements for many social work programs, which include previous experience, may be based more on an ideological commitment to an apprenticeship model of training than on hard evidence of the benefits of such experience.

Intellectual Ability

Studies of the intellectual abilities of social work students overall have found positive correlations between intelligence and academic success. A number of different indicators of intellectual ability have been found to predict social work performance. Grade-point averages (GPAs) have been found to predict successful student outcome (Bogo & Davin, 1989; Cunningham, 1982; Dunlap, 1979; Radin, Benbenishty, & Leon, 1982), as have faculty ratings of intellectual potential (Pfouts & Henley, 1977) and assessment of students' problem-solving ability (Fortune, 1984). Using scholarly productivity as an outcome measure, Rosen (1979) found that while scholarly potential, defined as GPA scores of Ph.D. students, failed to predict productivity, scores on Miller's Analogies Test, a measure of verbal intelligence, correlated positively with subsequent performance.

Measures on both verbal and mathematical subscales of intelligence tests were found to correlate with student ability to predict client responses (Plotnick, 1977). Measures of cognitive complexity were found to correlate with student ability to generate alternate responses to client problems (Duehn & Proctor, 1974) and to provide congruent responses to client verbalizations (Duehn & Mayadas, 1979).

Academic grades in social work courses, however, failed to predict subsequent job performance as rated by supervisors in a study by Cummins and

Arkava (1979). Student field-work evaluations, likewise, failed to predict clinical performance. The only significant association found with supervisor ratings were scores on a skill-based competency exam.

Several studies (Dailey, 1979; Dunlap, 1979; Pfouts & Henley, 1977) have used global faculty ratings of application materials, including academic records, reference letters, and personal statements, to predict student performance and/or to make admissions judgments. Such ratings generally were found to have low predictive validity for subsequent student achievement. Bogo and Davin (1989), for example, found that faculty assignment of *at-risk* status, indicating questionable or marginal suitability for social work based on subjective evaluations of students' personal statements, failed to predict subsequent student performance. Dailey (1974; 1979) concluded that a primary difficulty in using such ratings is their low interrater reliability. In one study of faculty ratings, the average interrater reliability was only $r = .22$, ranging from $r = -.62$ to $r = +.82$. Criteria used by different faculty members were as likely to be diverse as congruent, with the result that positive ratings cancelled out negative ones yielding a null effect.

In summary, the evidence to date consistently indicates that the best predictor of social work student performance is past academic performance. This is true whether the outcome criterion is clinical performance in the practicum or academic performance in the classroom. However, it is less clear whether past academic performance continues to predict clinical performance subsequent to graduation.

Psychological Characteristics

Evaluations of personality or psychological characteristics of social work students and their association with subsequent performance have produced mixed results. Hess and Williams (1974) compared social work students' personality scores to established test norms and found that social work students rated low on personal adjustment and affiliation and high on aggression. However, no comparison student group data were provided, and no statistical analysis was provided to demonstrate that these scores reflected significant variations from the norm.

Several studies have investigated the correlation of personality traits with student performance. Stein, Linn and Furdon (1974) found that low dogmatism, authoritarianism, and alienation scores at the beginning of social work training correlated positively with high faculty ratings at the end of the year. However, no correlation with field instruction ratings was observed. Jackson and Ahrons (1985) found a positive correlation between emotional sensitivity, evaluated on the basis of responses to a videotaped model, with subsequent ratings of interpersonal effectiveness by classroom peers. Davis and Sherman (1987) found student tolerance of ambiguity was positively correlated with social work students' grade averages. Assertiveness, in contrast, did not predict field-work performance (Cunningham, 1982).

Several studies have found negative correlations between students' psychological attributes and academic performance. Vigilante (1983) found that student self-preoccupation predicted subsequent learning problems in social work courses. However, faculty assessments served as the basis for both ratings, casting doubt on the independence of the measures. Plotnick (1977) found that intraception, or the tendency to make personal subjective evaluations, was negatively correlated with ability to predict client responses, whereas extraception, or the tendency to use impersonal, objective evaluations, was positively correlated with prediction.

Wodarski, Pippin, and Daniels (1988) studied changes in personality traits of both part- and full-time social work students over the course of training. No changes in personality traits were observed for the full-time students, whereas the part-time students became more extroverted over time.

The relative importance of personality traits and other student characteristics in predicting social work success has not been studied. Many of the positive traits that have been studied could be considered to comprise a general openness to new learning and new situations. These characteristics by definition are likely to correlate positively with learning, as well as with general intelligence. In summary, the case for any personality trait being a significant predictor of social work success has not yet been made.

Attitudes and Values

Studies of social work students' attitudes and values have investigated differences between social work students and other students as well as changes in social work students' attitudes and values over the course of their training. In the 1960s a series of studies by Varley (1963, 1968) and Hayes and Varley (1965), using the Social Work Questionnaire to measure values of equal rights, service, psychodynamic-mindedness, and universalism, failed to elicit any demonstrable differences between social work students and other students. Social work training tended to result in increased endorsement of equal rights, but decreased endorsement of the other values. A subsequent replication of Varley's studies by Judah (1979) substantially confirmed the earlier findings in that no changes in values were found, with the exception of universalism, which changed in the negative direction.

A variety of measures of other values have been used to elicit somewhat different results. Sharwell (1974), measuring attitudes toward public dependency, found that 20 beginning social work students had more positive attitudes than non-social work students. Retested at graduation, the social work students had become even more positive in their attitudes. However, because no comparison group was used, the observed change could not be attributed to social work training.

Using the same measure with a larger sample of students ($N = 367$), Merdinger (1982) found significantly more positive attitudes toward public dependency among social work students than among psychology and economics students. The social work students also scored higher than the economics students on altruism, trust, and independence.

Enoch (1988) compared 64 Israeli social work students with 75 social science students and found the former were more likely to support socialistic over capitalistic systems, to choose a vocation that had social importance and involved helping people or improving the country, and to score higher in faith in people, group responsibility to individuals, and individual rights for the fulfillment of basic needs. Studying a sample of social workers comprised mainly of students, Koeske and Crouse (1981) found that social workers had more liberal attitudes than the population at large.

In contrast to these findings, which suggest a high level of social consciousness among social work students, Carlton and Jung (1972) found that only 11% of social work students were interested in careers in grass-roots community service or social action settings. Similarly, a decade later, Rubin and Johnson (1984) found that the vast majority of students (86%) entering eight different schools of social work reported aspirations of entering private practice after graduation and planned to treat mildly disturbed clients with intensive psychotherapeutic methods. Only a small minority (14%) favored social interventive methods. In a later study comparing this baseline with attitudes at graduation, only a modest increment in espousal of social interventive methods was observed, and no change in the espousal of counseling methods was observed (Rubin, Johnson, & DeWeaver, 1986).

Lack of demonstrable change in student values and/or attitudes over the course of social work training has been the predominant finding, even when deliberate efforts to induce such changes have been implemented. Orten (1981) compared a group of students who engaged in poverty-living simulations with a comparison group of social work students. No differences between the two groups were found, despite the deliberate effort to influence attitudes toward poverty in the simulation group. While individual students in the experimental group did experience attitude changes, these changes occurred equally in positive and negative directions, effectively cancelling each other out in the aggregated results. Joseph and Conrad (1983) compared effects of teaching an ethics course, which involved self-examination of values and attitudes, with the more traditional integrated approach in which ethical content is diffused throughout the curriculum. Although individual attitudes or values were not assessed, the results indicated that both knowledge and the ability to apply knowledge to ethical decision-making improved significantly through the focused course approach.

Wodarski, Pippin, and Daniels (1988) investigated changes in social responsibility, responsibility for others, social values, and dogmatism in both full- and part-time students over the course of training. No significant changes were found among part-time students, and only one of the four measures, social values, changed significantly among full-time students.

One explanation for lack of changes observed was offered by Hepworth and Shumway, (1976) who found no significant changes on a dogmatism scale at the end of one year of training, but did find significant changes at the end of the second year. They suggested that a delayed response to social work training may exist. However, neither this study, nor two other studies demonstrating changes in values (O'Connor & Dalgleish, 1986; Sharwell, 1974), used comparison groups, so it is not possible to rule out effects of maturation or history and to attribute observed changes to training.

In summary, the conclusion reached by Orten (1981) that social work students, particularly those with minority and low SES backgrounds, begin social work training with somewhat different attitudes and values than other students and that these values are not significantly altered by training, has received considerable support in the empirical literature.

Attitudes Toward Research

A common assumption exists that social workers have a negative attitude toward research, but that effective research training can alter this in a positive direction. Neither the assumption of significantly negative attitudes or the ability to change attitudes through training, however, has received consistent empirical support. Basom, Iacono-Harris, and Kraybill (1982) compared social work and social science students' attitudes toward research at the beginning and end of an undergraduate statistics course. No differences between the two student groups were observed, and no significant attitude changes were found over the course of training. Linn and Greenwald (1974), in contrast, found that social work students assigned a negative rating to the concept of "researcher" at the beginning of training, but ratings of this concept changed significantly in the positive direction over the course of an academic year.

Two studies that compared social workers at different levels of training reported mixed results regarding attitudes toward research. Rosenblatt and Kirk (1981) compared BSW, MSW, and Ph.D. students and found that while the *importance* and *usefulness* of research was rated higher by each progressive level of education, there was no change in the perception of *validity* of research. Rosen and Mutschler (1982b) replicated this study and included social work practitioners in the sample. Practitioners' ratings were most similar to undergraduate students' ratings, in being significantly less positive than graduate students' ratings. It was suggested that the negative attitudes of practitioners reflected the failure of the social work research curriculum to address the realities of practice.

Biggerstaff and Kolevzon (1980) investigated differences between social work practitioners with different levels of training and found that *assessing client effect,* a research-based skill, was the only factor that discriminated across three levels of training. The importance accorded to this factor significantly increased with each increment in training level.

Several studies have investigated the effect of combined research-practice courses, or empirically based practice, on attitudes toward and subsequent use of research. Siegel (1983) found an overall increase in negative attitudes toward research across several sections of practice-research courses. In a subsequent analysis, Siegel (1985) demonstrated that the variance in scores was largely attributable to differences among sections, indicating that instruction differentially affected attitudes, but in an unknown manner.

Simons (1987) evaluated the extent to which students utilized empirically based practice principles at the end of training and nine months posttraining compared to a pretraining baseline. Results indicated significant posttraining increments in endorsement of empirical validation of practice theory, use of empirically based practice approaches, belief in operationalization of problems, and use of measurement and graphs to monitor progress. However, at nine-month follow-up, these increments were dissipating at varying rates with the extent of dissipation correlating with employment setting. The conclusion drawn was that colleagues' attitudes and environmental supports were more important than training in influencing attitudes and behaviors toward social work research.

Values and attitudes in social work students have not been shown to be easily influenced by training. Environmental factors, such as students' previous backgrounds or their subsequent employment situations, appear to have stronger and more direct bearing on their attitudes than training or educational experiences. Negative attitude changes appear to be as prevalent as positive changes. It has been suggested that training frequently involves the dissolution of naive altruistic intentions and their replacement with a more realistic appraisal of the difficulties of providing effective client service. Further variables within the delivery of educational programs may affect this process.

PROGRAM DELIVERY

Length and Level of Training

Variations in social work training programs that have been studied include full- versus part-time programs and accelerated (advanced standing) versus regular training programs. Typically, these studies have failed to demonstrate significant differences between programs.

Four studies comparing part- and full-time studies found no differences in the academic or field practicum performance of students (Davis, Short, & York, 1984; Kramer, Mathews, & Endias, 1987; Starr & Walker, 1982; Yamatani, Page, Koeske, Diaz, & Maguire, 1986). Different experiences of stress were reported in one study, with full-time students experiencing more financial stress and part-time students experiencing more stress in their work situations and with school personnel (Kramer, Mathews, & Endias, 1987).

Comparisons of accelerated or advanced-standing students with regular students similarly have yielded mixed results. Richman and Rosenfeld (1988) found no differences between two-year MSW students and advanced standing (BSW plus one-year MSW) students in student ratings of satisfaction or job preparedness. Two-year MSW students were significantly more likely to report that their program was too long. Kadushin and Kelling (1977) found no differences between three-year undergraduate versus traditional four-year BA programs in successful MSW completion. In a Canadian study, no differences in MSW classroom or practicum outcomes were found between BA and BSW students (Herington, Knoll, & Thomlison, 1981). Schlessinger and Wolock (1974) found only one difference, superior performance in Human Behavior courses, between 2-year and 16-month MSW students. O'Neil (1980) compared accelerated one-year MSW students with two-year MSW students and found the accelerated students were younger, less experienced, had higher grade point averages, and a greater sense of competence, but received lower ratings of practice competence by supervisors. No evaluation of academic performance was reported.

In contrast, negative findings regarding BSW-prepared, as compared to BA-prepared, MSW social workers were reported in two studies. Specht, Britt, and Frost (1984) found that, five years after completion of their MSW degree, employment status, salary, and participation in continuing and advanced educational programs were significantly higher for BA-prepared social workers. Similarly benefits in terms of cognitive development, as measured on scales of dualism, empathy, and attitude about reality, were found among BA-prepared students in an MSW program (Harrison, Kwong, & Cheong, 1989). These studies suggest that the more comprehensive undergraduate preparation afforded by the BA degree, which includes more exposure to English and the humanities, has benefits for professional development, which have not been recognized in outcome studies that focused on academic standing or student satisfaction alone.

In summary, research to date has provided little support for the superiority of the traditional full-time, two-year postgraduate MSW training program in terms of academic outcomes of students. Innovative arrangements, including various models of part-time and accelerated study, have yielded outcomes that were not substantially different from the traditional full-time model. However, when continued professional development was studied as the outcome variable, support for the benefits of more comprehensive undergraduate preparation was apparent.

Directed Field Studies

A number of variations in student practica have been investigated. Qualifications of practica supervisors were investigated in two studies, neither of which was able to document the hypothesized superiority of MSW supervisors. Smith and Baker (1989) studied MSW, MA, BSW, and BA supervisors and found no differences among them on the basis of student ratings. Field faculty, however, rated both MSW and MA supervisors as superior in providing high-quality supervision. Thyer, Williams, Love, and Sowers-Hoag (1989), in a retrospective analysis of student ratings of field supervisors, found no differences between MSW and other supervisors. They also cited a 1982 study by Raskin that found MSW supervisors were rated lower than non-MSW supervisors. On the basis of student evaluations, little support has been found for the superiority of MSW supervisors. It is likely that supervisor traits other than educational level are more important in determining the quality of practicum supervision offered.

Differences between paid or work-study and traditional practicum arrangements were studied by Abbott (1986). Student evaluations revealed no significant differences in levels of satisfaction. Work-study students, however, reported receiving significantly greater numbers of supervision hours.

Delayed placement, which followed a skill-training program, was compared with traditional immediate placement in a 1969 study by Gordon and Gordon (1989). The conclusion reached in the original study, that there were no differences between the two arrangements, was considered equally valid in their discussion of the study 20 years later.

Ramsey (1989) investigated differences between delivery of practica as a block, currently with classes, or as a concurrent block (4 days field, 1 day class). The dependent variable was practice orientation, defined as either theoretical or practical. Findings indicated that students in block placements were more likely to develop practical orientations, whereas students in concurrent placements were more likely to develop theoretical orientations. Whether these orientations had any effects on student performance, however, was not determined.

In summary, varieties of practica have primarily been studied in terms of student satisfaction or their effects on student practice orientations with no determination of other types of outcome. Qualifications of supervisors appear to favor graduate over undergraduate qualifications with no difference between social work and non-social work training. Evidence regarding work-study or paid placements and variations in practicum scheduling to date have failed to elicit different outcomes of these variations.

EDUCATORS

Social work educators have been evaluated primarily in relation to the academic criteria of educational qualifications, publication, and involvement in research. Little attention has been paid to the effect of educator variables on student performance.

Productivity of social work educators, defined in terms of numbers of publications, has been studied and found to be correlated individually with Ph.D. qualifications and collectively with schools providing Ph.D. training (Brownstein, 1985; Faver, Fox, Hunter, & Shannon, 1986; Jayaratne, 1979; Thyer & Bentley, 1986). Although the academic qualifications of faculty have been found to predict publication rates, less evidence has been found that such qualifications affect student learning. In a comparison of social work faculty with non-social work faculty teaching a Human Behavior course, Sze, Kella, and Kella (1979) found no differences in outcome on student knowledge, ability to apply knowledge to practice, or human relations awareness.

Tenure was found to be correlated with productivity as well as satisfaction by McNeece (1981). More positive attitudes toward research were found among untenured faculty in a more recent study (Faver, Fox, Hunter, & Shannon, 1986).

Effects of educators on student performance were evaluated in a study by Tolson & Kopp (1988) that investigated the transfer of knowledge and skills from classroom to field. Theoretical orientations of classroom practice instructors were found to be significantly related to both the average number of student interviews per client completed in the field and the number of interventions per interview. Students with task-centered instructors had the fewest number of interviews; students with interactional instructors had more interviews; and students with cognitive-behavioral or psychodynamic instructors had the greatest number of interviews. Students with task-centered instructors were found to have the highest rates of interventions per interview, perhaps due to the shorter intervention time anticipated.

Knowledge about effects of educator characteristics on the training of clinical practitioners has remained scarce. Academic criteria have greater saliency for faculty member careers than for student outcomes, and this bias has been reflected in the empirical literature. Variations in teaching methods, however, have received considerably more attention.

TEACHING METHODS

The research on teaching general therapeutic skills has focused largely on three types of training: didactic-experiential, microtraining, and behavioral training. In addition, there has been substantial research on the specific components within the training methods, namely role-play, modeling, supervisor, and video-feedback (Matarazzo & Patterson, 1986). Research on teaching clinical skills in social work has encompassed these topics, with somewhat less emphasis on behavioral training. Although research on specific training approaches has been relatively abundant within the field of social work itself, a review of interpersonal skill training by Marshall, Charping, and Bell (1979) noted that only 1 of 122 studies reported between

1968 and 1978 appeared in a social work journal. The present review, however, located more than 25 studies that reported empirical investigation of training methods in social work journals. Trends in social work training were found to be similar to trends in psychotherapy training; early studies focused on didactic-experiential approaches, and more recent studies focused on the microtraining model.

Didactic-Experiential Training

Truax and Carkhuff (1967) developed and expanded the didactic-experiential training model originally expounded by Rogers (1975) and based on the facilitative therapeutic conditions of empathy, genuineness, and nonpossessive warmth. The instructional program initiated by Rogers and developed by Truax and Carkhuff included extensive reading, listening to model tapes, and role playing with supervisory feedback in addition to regular group supervision. This model has generated a great deal of research in both psychotherapy and social work training.

An early study by Keefe (1975) investigated empathic sensitivity among social work students and found that graduate students were significantly more sensitive than undergraduates and that female students were more sensitive than males. No correlations of sensitivity with grade point average or micro/macro specialization, however, were observed. In a subsequent study Keefe (1979) compared didactic-experiential methods with mediation in developing empathic sensitivity. No significant increment in sensitivity was found for either method over control levels. This study, however, was criticized for not using equivalent comparison groups (Hepworth, 1980). A subsequent replication by Corcoran (1982), using Carkhuff's Empathic Understanding Scale in addition to affective sensitivity measures, found that both methods resulted in significantly greater increments in empathy over no-training controls.

Larsen and Hepworth (1978) utilized both Truax and Carkhuff's training model and measures to rate student performance and compared them to students trained with traditional didactic methods. While both groups made significant gains in their response levels, the students who received didactic-experiential training made significantly greater gains than students who received didactic training alone. Fischer (1975) similarly found significantly greater increments in student attainment of facilitative conditions with training as compared to attention and no-contact controls. The benefits of training were reflected in higher practicum supervisor ratings of student facilitative skill and self-actualization, but not in ratings of student effectiveness or overall practicum performance.

Toseland and Spielberg (1982) evaluated a didactic-experiential approach to teaching 10 interpersonal skills to undergraduate students in social work. Compared to social welfare majors who received no training, the studied group improved significantly on paper-and-pencil measures of discrimination and communication of skills. The authors warned, however, that the students, who typically began training with very low skill levels, improved only to minimally helpful levels after 45 hours of training.

Although these social work studies demonstrated the potential of the didactic-experiential approach for improving clinician facilitative conditions as rated by objective measures, evidence was accumulating in the psychotherapy literature that these measures did not always correlate with clients' feelings of being understood or helped. Instead, the measures frequently correlated with other aspects of clinician responding, such as the number of utterances, use of emotionally descriptive terms, and global measures of clinician competence (Matarazzo & Patterson, 1986). A focus on behavioral skills and behavioral ratings of skill acquisition, therefore, subsequently developed in both social work and psychotherapy training studies.

Microtraining

Much of the training in interviewing skills has been based on Ivey and colleagues' (1968) microcounseling approach, which addresses skills individually in terms of their behavioral components. The skill of attending, for example, has been defined as consisting of appropriate eye contact, body language, verbal encouragement, and paraphrasing. Microtraining for attending includes didactic presentations, modeling, videotaped practice with self-confrontation, supervisor feedback, and further practice. In general, studies of microtraining have demonstrated positive skill increments over no-training controls (Matarazzo & Patterson, 1986).

A number of clinical training studies in social work have evaluated the microtraining model, or components thereof, and compared it to more traditional training approaches. Taubman (1978) compared the effects of a single videotaped self-confrontation to a role-play and to didactic teaching. No differences on skills of exploration responses, active listening, attention to affect, and honest labelling were found. However, the training consisted of only one 40-minute session. Star (1977) similarly studied one videotaping experience but supplemented it with three playback experiences. Significant changes in perceptions of self as helper and inferred client perceptions were found after self-confrontation in the first feedback, but these changes diminished over subsequent feedback sessions.

Mayadas and Duehn (1977) compared process recording, videotaped feedback, and modeling plus supervisory feedback in the acquisition of questioning, reflecting, and expressing skills. Process recording produced the least change in skills. Modeling produced significantly greater change in reflection skills and in content expression skills than the other methods, and videotaped feedback produced significantly greater changes in affect expression and content reflection than process recording or modeling. The authors concluded that modeling, generally, was the most effective training method because it provided a greater number of external cues to facilitate student learning, which was particularly useful to less capable students.

A composite training model that included modeling, role play, feedback, and reinforcement was assessed by Schinke, Smith, Gilchrist, and Wong (1978), who found significant improvements in posture, questioning, and summarization skills over no-training controls. In a subsequent quasi-experimental study, skill acquisition acquired under such training was found to generalize to performance in field practica (Schinke, Blythe, Gilchrist, & Smith, 1980). Rose and Edleson (1979) similarly found significant increments in total skills among trained students compared to waiting list controls. And LeCroy (1982) reported skill increments in a longitudinal study of students in which controls were not used.

Advanced students have been used to provide microtraining to beginning students in several studies. Kurtz, Marshall, and Holloway (1982) noted changes in both trainers and trainees in such a program. Trainers were found to demonstrate significant increments in attending skills over a comparison peer group, while trainees attained skill levels equivalent to those of the trainers or advanced students generally. Rivas and Toseland (1981) reported an analogous training program for group work skills in which senior students, who led groups of junior students, reported significant pre- and post-training changes in 11 out of 15 group leader skills. No control or comparison groups, however, were utilized.

A number of studies have investigated brief training programs for social work practitioners. The training of 69 caseworkers in the task-centered approach was evaluated by Shapiro, Mueller-Lazar, and Witkin (1980). One group was provided with modeling plus role plays, while the comparison group received role plays alone. Greater increments in skills of setting time limits, developing tasks, dividing work on tasks, and summarizing content were observed in the modeling-plus-role-play group, but no statistical tests to examine the significance of the differences were computed. Furthermore, initial differences between the two groups were noted. A subsequent study by Rooney (1985) evaluated task-centered training using a paper-and-pencil analogue test, worker self-reports, and client questionnaires. Training resulted in significantly higher ratings of analogue responses and in client reports of higher agreement with treatment plan, identifying problem, and setting time limits. In contrast, no training effects were reported by Reid and Beard (1980) for a task-centered approach applied as an in-service program. Inspection of pretraining performance, however, suggested that practitioners were already using various components of this approach, leaving little room for improvement.

Two studies have evaluated training for family and children's workers, but neither used comparison or control groups to determine training effects. Lindsey, Yarbrough, and Morton (1981) evaluated a skill training program using pre- versus post-training comparisons and observed gains in attending behaviors, reflection, and global ratings of empathy and genuineness. A similar short-term training program, evaluated by Amatea, Munson, Anderson, and Rudner (1980), showed increments in interviewing skills, which failed to reach statistical significance on pre- and post-training comparisons. However, self-reports of competence and use of family perspective increased significantly over baseline measures.

SUMMARY

Research has shown that both didactic-experiential training and microtraining are more effective in producing desired results than no training or more traditional didactic teaching methods. The experiential element in learning clinical skills, including role-play, modeling, and either supervisory or video feedback, has been shown to be important in improving clinical behavior. This experiential element, furthermore, has received consistently high ratings by participating students (Brennen & Arkava, 1974; Viccaro, 1978).

The extent to which simulated training exercises generalize to clinical settings and the extent to which clients benefit from such training has received limited study. Rooney (1985) found that clients perceived differences in clinician task-centered behavior following training, but Barber (1988) failed to find differences in client ratings following microtraining. However, Barber's criteria of ratings of clinician expertness, attractiveness, and trustworthiness did not evaluate the specific microskills that were part of the training program.

In summary, training methods that focus on specific skills or that delineate and reward the use of specific clinical behaviors have been found to result in student gains. Students have been found to be more empathetic as a result of experiential-didactic training and more attentive as a result of microtraining. However, the extent to which these student gains translate into client benefits has not been determined.

REFERENCES

Abbott, A. A. (1986). The field placement contract: Its use in maintaining comparability between employment-related and traditional field placements. *Journal of Social Work Education, 22,* 57-66.

Abramowitz, C. V., Abramowitz, S. I., Roback, H. B., & Jackson, C. (1974). Differential effectiveness of directive and nondirective group therapies as a function of client internal-external control. *Journal of Consulting and Clinical Psychology, 42,* 849-853.

Alcabes, A., & Jones, J. A. (1985). Social work assessment: Route to clienthood. Part I. *Social Casework, 66,* 49-53.

Alexander, L. B., & Simon, A. (1973). Fischer's study of studies. *Social Work, 18,* 4-5.

Alperin, R. M., & Neidengarad, T. H. (1984). Effects of practitioners' professional affiliation, sex, and warmth on changes in the attitudes of clients. *Social Work Research & Abstracts, 20,* 20-26.

Amatea, E. S., Munson, P. A., Anderson, L. M., & Rudner, R. A. (1980). A short-term training program for caseworkers in family counseling. *Social Casework, 61,* 205-214.

American Psychiatric Association. (1987). *Diagnostic and statistical manual of mental disorders* (3rd ed., rev.). Washington, DC: Author.

Anderson, C. M., Reiss, D. J., & Hogarty, C. E. (1985). *Schizophrenia in the family: A practitioners' guide to psychoeducation and management.* New York: Guilford.

Anderson, S. A., Atiliano, R. B., Bergen, L. P., Russell, C. S., & Jurich, A. P. (1985). Dropping out of marriage and family therapy: Intervention strategies and spouses' perceptions. *American Journal of Family Therapy, 13,* 39-54.

Anderson, S. C., & Mandell, D. L. (1989). The use of self-disclosure by professional social workers. *Social Casework, 70,* 259-267.

Auslander, G. K., & Litwin, H. (1987). The parameters of network interventions: A social work application. *Social Service Review, 61,* 305-318.

Baekeland, F., & Lundwall, L. (1975). Dropping out of treatment: A critical review. *Psychological Bulletin, 82,* 738-783.

Bagarozzi, D. A., & Giddings, C. W. (1983). Behavioral marital therapy: Empirical status, current practices, trends and future directions. *Clinical Social Work Journal, 11,* 263-279.

Baker, D. R., & Smith, S. L. (1988). A comparison of field faculty and field student perceptions of selected aspects of supervision. *The Clinical Supervisor, 5,* 31-42.

Barber, J. (1988). Are microskills worth teaching? *Journal of Social Work Education, 24,* 3-12.

Barlow, D. H., Hayes, S. C., & Nelson, R. D. (1984). *The scientist practitioner: Research and accountability in clinical and educational settings.* New York: Pergamon.

Basom, R. E., Iacono-Harris, D. A., & Kraybill, D. B. (1982). Statistically speaking: Social work students are significant. *Journal of Education for Social Work, 18,* 20-26.

Baucom, D. H., & Hoffman, J. A. (1986). The effectiveness of marital therapy: Current status and application to the clinical setting. In N. S. Jacobson & A. S. Gurman (Eds.), *Clinical handbook of marital therapy* (pp. 597-621). New York: Guilford.

Beck, D. F. (1975). Research findings on the outcomes of marital counseling. *Social Casework, 56,* 153-181.

Beck, D. F. (1987a). Counselor burnout in family service agencies. *Social Casework, 68,* 3-15.

Beck, D. F. (1978b). *Counselor characteristics: How they affect outcomes.* NY: Family Services Association of America.

Beck, D. F., & Jones, M. A. (1973). *Progress on family problems: A nationwide study of clients' and counselors' views on family agency services.* New York: Family Services Association of America.

Beck, D. F., & Jones, M. A. (1974). A new look at clientele and services of family agencies. *Social Casework, 55,* 589-599.

Becker, N. E., & Becker, F. W. (1986). Early identification of high social risk. *Health and Social Work, 11,* 26-35.

Bednar, R. L., & Kaul, T. J. (1978). Experiential group research: Current perspectives. In S. L. Garfield & A. E. Bergin (Eds.), *Handbook of psychotherapy and behavior change* (2nd ed., pp. 769-816). New York: Wiley.

Behling, J. C., Curtis, C., & Foster, S. A. (1982). Impact of sex-role combinations of student performance in field instruction. *Journal of Education for Social Work, 18,* 93-97.

Beinecke, R. H. (1984). PORK, SOAP, STRAP and SAP. *Social Casework, 65,* 554-558.

Berg, D. N., & Smith, K. K. (Eds.). (1985). *Exploring clinical methods for social research.* Beverly Hills: Sage.

Berg, W. E. (1980). Effects of job satisfaction on practice decisions. A linear flow-graph analysis. *Social Work Research & Abstracts, 16,* 30-37.

Berger, R., & Piliavin, I. (1976). The effect of casework: A research note. *Social Work, 21,* 205-208.

Bergin, A. E., & Garfield, S. L. (1971). *Handbook of psychotherapy and behavior change.* New York: Wiley.

Bergin, A. E., & Garfield, S. L. (1986). *Handbook of psychotherapy and behavior change.* (3rd ed.). New York: Wiley.

Bergin, A. E., & Lambert, J. J. (1978). The evaluation of therapeutic outcomes. In S. L. Garfield & A. E. Bergin (Eds.), *The handbook of psychotherapy and behavior change: An empirical analysis* (pp. 139-198). New York: Wiley.

Berkman, B. (1980). Psychosocial problems and outcomes: An external validity study. *Health and Social Work, 5,* 5-21.

Berkman, B., Bedell, D., Parker, E., McCarthy, L., & Rosenbaum, C. (1988). Preadmission screening: An efficacy study. *Social Work in Health Care, 13,* 35-50.

Berkman, B., Dumas, S., Gastfriend, J., Poplawski, J., & Southworthe, M. (1987). Predicting hospital readmission of elderly cardiac patients. *Health and Social Work, 13,* 221-228.

Berkman, B. G., & Rehr, H. (1970). Unanticipated consequences of casefinding system in hospital social service. *Social Work, 15,* 63-68.

Berkman, B. G., & Rehr, H. (1973). Early social service casefinding for hospitalized patients: An experiment. *Social Service Review, 47,* 256-265.

Berkman, B., & Rehr, H. (1978). Social work undertakes its own audit. *Social Work in Health Care, 3,* 273-286.

Berlin, S. (1980). Cognitive-behavioral interventions for problems of self-criticism among women. *Social Work Research & Abstracts, 16,* 19-28.

Berlin, S. (1985). Maintaining reduced levels of self-criticism through relapse-prevention treatment. *Social Work Research & Abstracts, 21,* 21-33.

Beutler, L. E. (1981). Convergence in counseling and psychotherapy: A current look. *Clinical Psychology Review, 1,* 79-101.

Beutler, L. E., Crago, M., & Arizmendi, T. G. (1986). Research on therapist variables in psychotherapy. In S. L. Garfield & A. E. Bergin (Eds.), *Handbook of psychotherapy and behavior change* (3rd ed., pp. 257-310). New York: Wiley.

Biggerstaff, M. A., & Kolevzon, M. S. (1980). Differential use of social work knowledge, skill and techniques by MSW, BSW and BA level practitioners. *Journal of Education for Social Work, 16,* 67-74.

Billups, J. O., & Julia, M. C. (1987). Changing profile of social work practice: A content analysis. *Social Work Research & Abstracts, 23,* 17-22.

Blau, P. M. (1960). Orientation toward clients in a public welfare agency. *Administrative Sciences Quarterly, 5,* 341-361.

Bleckner, M., Bloom, M., & Nielsen, M. (1971). A research and demonstration project of protective services. *Social Casework, 52,* 483-499.

Blizinsky, M. J., & Reid, W. J. (1980). Problem focus and change in a brief treatment model. *Social Work, 25,* 89-93.

Bloom, M. (1976). An analysis of the research on educating social work students. *Journal of Education for Social Work, 12,* 3-10.

Bloom, M. (1983). Empirically based clinical practice. In A. Rosenblatt & D. Waldfogel (Eds.), *Handbook of clinical social work* (pp. 560-582). San Francisco: Jossey-Bass.

Bloom, M., & Block, S. R. (1977). Evaluating one's own effectiveness and efficiency. *Social Work, 22,* 130-137.

Bloom, M., Butch, P., & Walker, D. (1979). Evaluation of single interventions. *Journal of Social Service Research, 2,* 301-310.

Bloom, M., & Fischer, J. (1982). *Evaluating practice: Guidelines for the accountable professional.* Englewood Cliffs, NJ: Prentice-Hall.

Blumberg, D. D., Ely, A. R., & Kerbeshian, A. (1975). Clients' evaluation of medical services. *Social Work, 20,* 45-57.

Boettcher, R. E. (1977). Interspousal empathy, marital satisfaction and marital counseling. *Journal of Social Service Research, 1,* 105-113.

Bogo, M., & Davin, C. (1989). The use of admissions criteria and a practice skills measure in predicting academic and practicum performance of MSW students. *Canadian Social Work Review, 6,* 95-109.

Boone, C. R., Coulton, C. J., & Keller, S. M. (1982). Impact of early and comprehensive social work services on length of stay. *Social Work in Health Care, 7,* 1-9.

Borenzweig, H. (1981). Agency vs. private practice: Similarities and differences. *Social Work, 26,* 239-244.

Borkowski, M., Murch, M., & Walker, L. V. (1983). *Marital violence: The community response.* London: Tavistock.

Borland, J., & Jones, A. (1980). Referral patterns for social work services in ambulatory care settings. *Journal of Applied Social Services, 5,* 19-33.

Bostwick, G. J. (1987). "Where's Mary?" A review of the group drop-out literature. *Social Work with Groups, 10,* 117-132.

Bowker, L. H. (1984). Coping with wife abuse: Personal and social networks. In A. R. Roberts (Ed.), *Battered women and their families.* New York: Springer.

Bradmiller, L. L. (1978). Self-disclosure in the helping relationship. *Social Work Research & Abstracts, 14,* 28-35.

Brennen, E. C., & Arkava, M. L. (1974). Students view the undergraduate curriculum. *Journal of Education for Social Work, 10,* 9-16.

Breslau, N. (1982). Continuity reexamined: Differential impact on satisfaction with medical care for disabled and normal children. *Medical Care, 20,* 347-358.

Briar, S. (1961). Use of theory in studying effects of client social class on students' judgments. *Social Work, 6,* 91-97.

Brigg, E. H., & Mudd, E. H. (1968). An exploration of methods to reduce broken first appointments. *The Family Coordinator, 17,* 41-46.

Brown, C. R., & Hellinger, M. L. (1975). Therapists' attitudes toward women. *Social Work, 20,* 266-270.

Brown, G. W. (1987). Social factors and the development and course of depressive disorders in women: A review of a research program. *British Journal of Social Work, 17,* 615-634.

Brown, L. N. (1984). Mutual help staff groups to manage worker stress. *Social Work with Groups, 7,* 55-66.

Brown, R. A. (1973). Feedback in family interviewing. *Social Work, 18,* 52-59.

Brownstein, C. D. (1985). The social work educator: Social worker and professor? *Social Service Review, 59,* 496-504.

Buffum, W. E., & Konick, A. (1982). Employees' job satisfaction, resident's functioning and treatment progress in psychiatric institutions. *Health and Social Work, 7,* 320-327.

Burden, D. S., & Gottlieb, N. (1987). *The woman client. Providing human services in a changing world.* New York: Tavistock.

Camasso, M. J., & Camasso, A. E. (1986). Social support, undesirable life events and psychological distress in a disadvantaged population. *Social Service Review, 60,* 378-394.

Campbell, J. A. (1988). Client acceptance of single-system evaluation procedures. *Social Work Research & Abstracts, 24,* 21-22.

Canton, C. (1981). The new chronic patient and the system of community care. *Hospital and Community Psychiatry, 32,* 477.

Caputi, M. A., & Heiss, W. A. (1984). The DRG Revolution. *Health and Social Work, 9,* 5-12.

Carlton, T. O., & Jung, M. (1972). Adjustment or change: Attitudes among social workers. *Social Work, 17,* 64-71.

Caron, C., Corcoran, K. J., & Simcoe, F. (1983). Interpersonal correlates of burnout: The role of locus of control in burnout and self-esteem. *The Clinical Supervisor, 1,* 53-62.

Chandler, S. M. (1980). Self-perceived competency in cross-cultural counseling. *Social Casework, 61,* 347-353.

Cheatham, J. M. (1987). The empirical evaluation of clinical practice: A survey of four groups of practitioners. *Journal of Social Service Research, 10,* 163-177.

Cherniss, C. (1980). *Professional burnout in human service organizations.* New York: Praeger.

Cherniss, C., & Egnatios, E. (1978). Clinical supervision in community mental health. *Social Work, 23,* 219-223.

Christ, W. (1984). Factors delaying discharge of psychiatric patients. *Health and Social Work, 9,* 178-187.

Clinical Social Work Council. (1984). Definition of clinical social work. *N.A.S.W. News.*

Cocozelli, C. (1986). A psychometric study of the theoretical orientations of clinical social workers. *Journal of Social Service Research, 9,* 47-70.

Cocozelli, C. (1987). Testing typological hypotheses about clinical social work practice theory. *Journal of Social Work Education, 23,* 6-15.

Cocozelli, C., & Constable, R. T. (1985). An empirical analysis of the relation between theory and practice in clinical social work. *Journal of Social Service Research, 9,* 47-64.

Cohen, J. (1979). The nature of clinical social work. In P. L. Ewalt (Ed.), *Toward a definition of clinical social work* (pp. 23-32). Washington, DC: NASW.

Corcoran, J. J. (1982). Behavioral and nonbehavioral methods of developing two types of empathy: A comparative study. *Journal of Education for Social Work, 18,* 85-93.

Corcoran, J. J. (1987). The association of burnout and social work practitioners' impressions of their clients: Empirical evidence. *Journal of Social Service Research, 10,* 57-65.

Corcoran, J. J., & Bryce, A. K. (1984). Intervention in the experience of burnout: Effects of skill development. *Journal of Social Service Research, 7,* 71-79.

Corcoran, J. J., & Fischer, J. (1987). *Measures for clinical practice: A sourcebook.* New York: The Free Press.

Corrigan, E. M. (1980). New knowledge and the drinking woman: A contemporary view. In E. Norman & A. Mancuso (Eds.), *Women's issues and social work practice* (pp. 133-152). Itasca, IL: Peacock.

Couchon, W. D., & Bernard, J. M. (1984). Effects of timing of supervision on supervisor and counselor performance. *The Clinical Supervisor, 2,* 3-20.

Coulton, C. J. (1984). Confronting prospective payment: Requirements for an information system. *Health and Social Work, 9,* 13-24.

Coulton, C. J. (1985). Research and practice: An ongoing relationship. *Health and Social Work, 10,* 282-291.

Coulton, C. J. (1988). Evaluating screening and early intervention: A puzzle with many pieces. *Social Work in Health Care, 13,* 35-50.

Courage, M. M., & Williams, D. D. (1987). An approach to the study of burnout in professional care providers in human service organizations. *Journal of Social Service Research, 10,* 7-22.

Cousins, P. S., Fischer, J., Glisson, C., & Kameoka, V. (1986). The effects of physical attractiveness and verbal expressiveness on clinical judgments. *Journal of Social Service Research, 8,* 59-74.

Cowger, C. D. (1980). Social group work educators: Factors associated with literature preferences. *Social Work with Groups, 3,* 87-94.

Coyne, J. C., & DeLongis, A. (1986). Going beyond social support: The role of social relationships and adaptation. *Journal of Consulting and Clinical Psychology, 54,* 454-460.

Cross, D. G., & Brown, D. (1983). Counselor supervision as a function of trainee experience: Analysis of specific behaviors. *Counselor Education & Supervision, 22,* 333-341.

Crotty, P., & Kulys, R. (1985). Social support networks: The views of schizophrenic clients and their significant others. *Social Work, 30,* 301-309.

Cryns, A. G. (1977). Social work education and student ideology: A multivariate study of professional socialization. *Journal of Education for Social Work, 13,* 44-51.

Cummins, D. E., & Arkava, M. L. (1979). Predicting posteducational job performance of BSW graduates. *Social Work Research & Abstracts, 15,* 33-40.

Cunningham, G. (1978). Workers' support of clients' problem-solving. *Social Work Research & Abstracts, 14,* 3-9.

Cunningham, M. (1982). Admissions variables and the prediction of success in an undergraduate fieldwork program. *Journal of Education for Social Work, 18,* 27-34.

Curiel, H., & Rosenthal, J. A. (1987). Comparing structure in student supervision by social work program level. *The Clinical Supervisor, 5,* 53-67.

Dailey, D. M. (1974). The validity of admissions predictions: Implications for social work education. *Journal of Education for Social Work, 10,* 12-19.

Dailey, D. M. (1979). The validity of admissions predictions: A replication study and implications for the future. *Journal of Education for Social Work, 15,* 14-22.

Dailey, D. M. (1980). Are social workers sexist? A replication. *Social Work, 25,* 46-50.

Dailey, D. M. (1983). Androgyny, sex-role stereotypes, and clinical judgment. *Social Work Research & Abstracts, 12,* 20-24.

Davenport, J., & Reims, N. (1978). Theoretical orientations and attitudes toward women. *Social Work, 23,* 306-309.

Davis, H. W., Short, J. S., & York, R. O. (1984). Achieving quality field instruction in part-time graduate social work programs. *The Clinical Supervisor, 2,* 45-54.

Davis, L. V. (1984). Beliefs of service providers about abused women and abusing men. *Social Work, 29,* 243-249.

Davis, L. V. (1985). Female and male voices in social work. *Social Work, 30,* 106-113.

Davis, L. V., & Carlson, B. E. (1981). Attitudes of service providers toward domestic violence. *Social Work Research & Abstracts, 17,* 34-39.

Davis, L. V., & Sherman, E. (1987). Intolerance of ambiguity and student performance in social work education. *Journal of Social Work Education, 23,* 16-23.

Davis, S. (1986). The "new young chronic" psychiatric patient: A study in Vancouver. *Social Work in Health Care, 11,* 87-100.

Davis-Sacks, M. L., Jayaratne, S., & Chess, W. A. (1985). A comparison of the effects of social support on the incidence of burnout. *Social Work, 30,* 240-244.

Day, P. J. (1979). Sex-role stereotypes and public assistance. *Social Service Review, 53,* 106-115.

Denoff, M. S. (1982). The differentiation of supportive functions among network members: An empirical inquiry. *Journal of Social Service Research, 5,* 45-59.

Dhooper, S. S. (1984). Social networks and support during the crisis of heart attack. *Health and Social Work, 9,* 294-303.

Dinnerman, M., Seaton, R., & Schlesinger, E. G. (1987). Surviving DRG's: New Jersey's social work experience with prospective payments. *Social Work in Health Care, 12,* 103-113.

Donnan, H. H., & Mitchell, H. D., Jr. (1979). Preferences for older versus younger counselors among a group of elderly persons. *Journal of Counseling Psychology, 26,* 513-518.

Donovan, R. J. (1987). Stress in the work place: A framework for research and practice. *Social Casework, 68,* 259-266.

Dorfman, R. A. (1988). Clinical social work: The development of a discipline. In R. A. Dorfman (Ed.), *Paradigms of clinical social work* (pp. 3-24). New York: Brunner/Mazel.

Dove, H. G., Schneider, K. C., & Gitelson, D. A. (1985). Identifying patients who need social work services: An interdisciplinary analysis. *Social Work, 30,* 214-218.

Duehn, W. D., & Mayadas, N. S. (1979). Starting where the client is: An empirical investigation. *Social Casework, 59,* 67-74.

Duehn, W. D., & Proctor, E. K. (1974). A study of cognitive complexity in the education for social work practice. *Journal of Education for Social Work, 10,* 20-26.

Dunlap, W. R. (1979). How effective are graduate social work admission criteria? *Journal of Education for Social Work, 15,* 96-102.

Dunkle, R. E., Poulschock, W., Silverstone, B., & Deimling, G. T. (1983). Protective services reanalyzed: Does casework help or harm? *Social Casework, 64,* 195-199.

Dyer, P. M. (1977). How professional is the BSW worker? *Social Work, 22,* 487-492.

Eichler, M. (1988). *Nonsexist research methods: A practical guide.* Winchester, MA: Allan & Unwin.

Eisikovits, Z., Meier, R., Guttmann, E., Shurka, E., & Levinstein, A. (1986). Supervision in ecological context: The relationship between the quality of supervision and the work and treatment environment. *Journal of Social Service Research, 8,* 37-57.

Eldridge, W. D. (1983). Practitioners and self-evaluation. *Social Casework, 64,* 426-430.

Ell, K. (1984). Social networks, social supports and health status: A review. *Social Service Review, 58,* 133-149.

Ell, K., & Haywood, L. J. (1985). Social support and recovery from mycardial infarction: A panel study. *Journal of Social Service Research, 7,* 1-19.

Enoch, Y. (1988). Why are they different? Background, occupational choice, institutional selection and attitudes of social work students. *Journal of Social Work Education, 24,* 165-174.

Epstein, W. M. (1983). Research biases. *Social Work, 28,* 77-78.

Ewalt, P. L. (1979). *Toward a definition of clinical social work.* Washington, D.C.: NASW.

Ewalt, P. L., & Kutz, J. (1976). An examination of advice giving as a therapeutic intervention. *Smith College Studies in Social Work, 47,* 3-19.

Eysenck, H. J. (1952). The effects of psychotherapy: An evaluation. *Journal of Consulting Psychology, 16,* 319-324.

Fanshel, D. (1976). Status differentials: Men and women in social work. *Social Work, 21,* 448-454.

Farber, B. A., & Heifetz, L. J. (1982). The process and dimensions of burnout in psychotherapists. *Professional Psychology, 13,* 293-301.

Faver, C. A., Fox, M. F., Hunter, M. S., & Shannon, C. (1986). Research and practice orientations of social work educators. *Social Work, 31,* 282-286.

Feldman, R. A. (1987). Group work knowledge and research: A two-decade comparison. *Social Work with Groups, 9,* 7-14.

Feldman, R. A., & Caplinger, J. E. (1977). Social work experience and client behavior change. *Journal of Social Service Research, 1,* 5-33.

Fike, D. F. (1980). Evaluating group intervention. *Social Work with Groups, 3,* 41-51.

Fischer, J. (1973). Is casework effective? A review. *Social Work, 18,* 5-20.

Fischer, J. (1975). Training for effective therapeutic practice. *Psychotherapy: Theory, Research & Practice, 12,* 118-123.

Fischer, J. (1976). *The effectiveness of social casework.* Springfield, IL: C. C. Thomas

Fischer, J. (1978). Does anything work? *Journal of Social Service Research, 3,* 213-243.

Fischer, J. (1981). The social work revolution. *Social Work, 26,* 199-207.

Fischer, J. (1983). Evaluation of social work effectiveness: Is positive evidence always good evidence? *Social Work, 28,* 74-77.

Fischer, J., Dulaney, D. D., Fazio, R. T., Hudak, M. T., & Zivotofsky, E. (1976). Are social workers sexist? *Social Work, 21,* 428-433.

Fischer, J., & Hudson, W. W. (1976). An effect of casework? Back to the drawing board. *Social Work, 21,* 327-349.

Fischer, J., & Miller, H. (1973). The effects of client race and social class on clinical judgments. *Clinical Social Work Journal, 1,* 100-109.

Fortune, A. E. (1979a). Communication in task-centered treatment. *Social Work, 24,* 390-396.

Fortune, A. E. (1979b). Problem-solving processes in task-centered treatment with adults and children. *Journal of Social Service Research, 2,* 357-371.

Fortune, A. E. (1981). Communication processes in social work practice. *Social Service Review, 55,* 93-128.

Fortune, A. E. (1984). Problem-solving ability of social work students. *Journal of Education for Social Work, 20,* 25-33.

Fortune, A. E. (1985). Planning duration and termination of treatment. *Social Service Review, 59,* 647-661.

Franklin, D. L. (1985). Differential clinical assessment: The influence of class and race. *Social Service Review, 59,* 44-61.

Franklin, D. L. (1986). Does client social class affect clinical judgment? *Social Casework, 67,* 424-432.

Fraser, M., & Hawkins, J. D. (1984). Social network analysis and drug misuse. *Social Service Review, 58,* 91-97.

Friedman, F. G. A., & Berg, L. K. (1978). Graduate students' judgments about clients: The effects of social class. *Journal of Education for Social Work, 14,* 45-51.

Gaines, T., & Stedman, J. M. (1981). Factors associated with dropping out of child and family treatment. *American Journal of Family Therapy, 9,* 45-51.

Galinsky, M. J., & Schopler, J. H. (1977). Warning: Groups may be dangerous. *Social Work, 22,* 89-93.

Gallo, F. (1982). Effects of social support networks on the health of the elderly. *Social Work in Health Care, 8,* 65-74.

Gallo, F. (1984). Social support networks and the health of elderly persons. *Social Work Research & Abstracts, 20,* 13-19.

Gambrill, E. D., & Barth, R. P. (1980). Single-case study designs revisited. *Social Work Research & Abstracts, 16,* 15-20.

Garber, L., Brenner, S., & Litwin, D. (1986). A survey of patient and family satisfaction with social services. *Social Work in Health Care, 11,* 13-23.

Garfield, S. L. (1978). Research on client variables in psychotherapy. In S. L. Garfield & A. E. Bergin (Eds.), *Handbook of psychotherapy and behavior change* (2nd ed., pp. 191-232). New York: Wiley.

Garfield, S. L. (1986). Research on client variables in psychotherapy. In S. L. Garfield & A. E. Bergin (Eds.), *Handbook of psychotherapy and behavior change* (3rd ed., pp. 213-256). New York: Wiley.

Garfield, S. L., & Bergin, A. E. (1978). *Handbook of psychotherapy and behavior change* (2nd ed.). New York: Wiley.

Garfield, S. L., & Bergin, A. E. (1986). *Handbook of psychotherapy and behavior change* (3rd ed.). New York: Wiley.

Geismar, L. L., & Wood, K. M. (1982). Evaluating practice: Science as faith. *Social Casework, 13,* 266-272.

Getz, H. G., & Miles, J. H. (1978). Women and peers as counselors: A look at client preferences. *Journal of College Student Personnel, 19,* 37-41.

Gibbons, J., Bow, I., & Butler, J. (1985). Task-centered social work after parasuicide. In E. M. Goldberg, J. Gibbons, & I. Sinclair (Eds.), *Problems, tasks and outcomes: The evaluation of task-centered casework in three settings* (pp. 169-247). London: Allen & Unwin.

Gibbons, J. S., Bow, I., Butler, J., & Powell, J. (1979). Client's reactions to task-centered casework: A follow-up study. *British Journal of Social Work, 9,* 203-215.

Gibbs, L. E., & Johnson, P. J. (1983). Computer assisted clinical decision making. *Journal of Social Service Research, 6*, 119-131.

Gillespie, D. F. (1982). Correlates of active and passive types of burnout. *Journal of Social Service Research, 4*, 1-15.

Gillespie, D. F., & Seaberg, J. R. (1977). Individual problem rating: A proposed scale. *Administration in Mental Health, 5*, 21-29.

Gillum, R. F., & Barsky, A. (1974). Diagnosis and management of patient noncompliance. *Journal of American Medical Association, 228*, 1563-1567.

Gingerich, W. J. (1984). Generalizing single-case evaluation from classroom to practice setting. *Journal of Education for Social Work, 20*, 74-82.

Gingerich, W. J., & Kirk, S. A. (1981). Sex bias in assessment: A case of premature exaggeration. *Social Work Research & Abstracts, 17*, 38-43.

Glisson, C. (1987). The group versus the individual as the unit of analysis in small group research. *Social Work with Groups, 9*, 15-30.

Glisson, C. A., & Hudson, W. W. (1981). Applied statistical misuse in educational research: An admissions criteria example. *Journal of Education for Social Work, 17*, 35-44.

Goldberg, E. M., Gibbons, J., & Sinclair, I. (1985). *Problems, tasks and outcomes. The evaluation of task-centered casework in three settings.* London: Allen & Unwin.

Goldberg, E. M., Stanley, S. J., & Kenrich, J. (1985). Task-centered casework in a probation setting. In E. M. Goldberg, J. Gibbons, & I. Sinclair (Eds.), *Problems, tasks and outcomes: The evaluation of task-centered casework in three settings* (pp. 89-166). London: Allen & Unwin.

Goldberg, G. S., Kantrow, R., Kremen, E., & Lauter, L. (1986). Spouseless, childless elderly women and their social supports. *Social Work, 31*, 104-112.

Goldstein, E. G. (1979). Knowledge base of clinical social work. In P. L. Ewalt (Ed.), *Toward a definition of clinical social work* (pp. 403-422). Washington, DC: NASW.

Goodban, N. (1985). The psychological impact of being on welfare. *Social Service Review, 59*, 403-422.

Gordon, B., & Rehr, H. (1969). Selectivity biases in delivery of hospital social services. *Social Service Review, 43*, 35-41.

Gordon, W. E., & Gordon, M. S. (1989). George Warren Brown's field instruction research project: An experimental design tested by empirical data. *The Clinical Supervisor, 7*, 15-28.

Gottlieb, N. (1980). Women and chemical dependency. In N. Gottlieb (Ed.), *Alternate social services for women* (pp. 111-131). New York: Columbia University Press.

Gould, K. H., & Kim, B. (1976). Salary inequities between men and women in schools of social work: Myth or reality? *Journal of Education for Social Work, 12*, 50-55.

Granvold, D. K. (1978). Training social work supervisors to meet organizational and worker objectives. *Journal of Education for Social Work, 14*, 38-45.

Green, R. G., & Kolevzon, M. S. (1982). A survey of family therapy practitioners. *Social Casework, 63*, 95-99.

Grey, A. L., & Dermody, H. E. (1972). Reports of casework failure. *Social Casework, 53*, 534-543.

Grinnell, R. M., Jr., & Kyle, N. S. (1975). Environmental modification: A study. *Social Work, 20*, 313-318.

Gropper, M. (1988). A study of the preferences of family practitioners and other primary care physicians in treating patients' psychosocial problems. *Social Work in Health Care, 13*, 75-91.

Grosser, R. C., & Block, S. R. (1983). Clinical social work practice in the private sector: A survey. *Clinical Social Work Journal, 11,* 245-262.

Gurman, A. S., & Kniskern, D. P. (1978). Research on marital and family therapy: Progress, perspectives and prospects. In S. L. Garfield & A. E. Bergin (Eds.), *Handbook of psychotherapy and behavior change: An empirical analysis* (2nd ed., pp. 817-902). New York: Wiley.

Gurman, A. S., Kniskern, D. P., & Pinsof, W. M. (1986). Research processes and outcome of marital and family therapy. In S. L. Garfield & A. E. Bergin (Eds.), *Handbook of psychotherapy and behavior change* (3rd ed., pp. 565-624). New York: Wiley.

Haley, J. (1980). *Leaving home: The therapy of disturbed young people.* New York: McGraw-Hill.

Hanrahan, P., & Reid, W. J. (1984). Choosing effective interventions. *Social Service Review, 58,* 244-253.

Hansen, J. C., Robins, T. H., & Grimes, J. (1982). Review of research in practicum supervision. *Counselor Education and Supervision, 21,* 15-24.

Harrison, W. D. (1980). Role strain and burnout in child-protective service workers. *Social Service Review, 54,* 31-44.

Harrison, W. D., Kwong, K., & Cheong, K. J. (1989). Undergraduate education and cognitive development of MSW students: A follow-up to Specht, Britt and Frost (1984). *Social Work Research & Abstracts, 25,* 15-19.

Hayes, D. D., & Varley, B. K. (1965). The impact of social work education on students' values. *Social Work, 10,* 40-46.

Haynes, K. S. (1983). Sexual differences in social work administrators' job satisfaction. *Journal of Social Service Research, 6,* 57-73.

Healy, J. (1981). Emergency rooms and psychosocial services. *Health and Social Work, 6,* 36-43.

Hedblom, J. E. (1988). Measuring inpatient psychosocial severity. A progress report on the development of an instrument. *Social Work in Health Care, 13,* 59-73.

Hefner, C. W., & Prochaska, J. A. (1984). Concurrent vs. conjoint marital therapy. *Social Work, 29,* 287-291.

Heineman, M. B. (1981). The obsolete scientific imperative in social work research. *Social Service Review, 55,* 371-397.

Heller, K., Swindle, R. W., & Dusenbury, L. (1986). Component social support processes: Comments and integration. *Journal of Consulting and Clinical Psychology, 54,* 466-470.

Hepworth, D. (1980). The development of empathic skill. *Journal of Education for Social Work, 16,* 122-124.

Hepworth, D. H., & Shumway, E. G. (1976). Changes in open-mindedness as a result of social work education. *Journal of Education for Social Work, 12,* 56-62.

Herington, W., Knoll, R. A., & Thomlison, R. J. (1981). The granting of advanced standing to BSW graduates entering Year II of an MSW program: The University of Toronto experience. *Canadian Journal of Social Work Education, 7,* 73-86.

Hersen, M., & Barlow, D. H. (1976). *Single case experimental designs: Strategies for behavior change.* New York: Pergamon.

Hess, D., & Williams, M. (1974). Personality characteristics and value stances of students in two areas of graduate study. *Journal of Education for Social Work, 10,* 42-49.

Himle, D. P., Jayaratne, S. D., & Chess, W. A. (1987). Gender differences in work stress among clinical social workers. *Journal of Social Service Research, 10,* 41-56.

Hoch, C., & Hemmans, G. C. (1987). Linking informal and formal help: Conflict along the continuum of care. *Social Service Review, 61,* 432-446.

Hollis, F. (1967). Explorations in the development of a typology of casework treatment. *Social Casework, 48,* 335-341.

Hollis, F. (1972). *Casework* (2nd ed.). New York: Random House.

Home, A., & Darveau-Fournier, L. (1982). A study of social work practice with groups. *Social Work with Groups, 5,* 19-34.

Hopps, J. G. (1987). Who's setting social work's priorities? *Social Work, 32,* 99-100.

Howe, M. W. (1974). Casework self-evaluation: A single-study approach. *Social Service Review, 48,* 1-23.

Hudson, W. W. (1982). *The clinical measurement package: A field manual.* Homewood, IL: Dorsey.

Ivanoff, A., Blythe, B. J., & Briar, S. (1987). The empirical clinical practice debate. *Social Casework, 68,* 290-298.

Ivey, A. E. (1971). *Microcounseling: Innovations in interviewing training.* Springfield, IL: C. C. Thomas.

Ivey, A. E., Normington, C. J., Miller, D. C., Morrill, W. H., & Haase, R. F. (1968). Microcounseling and attending behavior: An approach to prepracticum counselor training. *Journal of Counseling Psychology Monograph* (Supp, 15, No. 5).

Jackson, E., & Ahrons, C. (1985). The relationship of practice area specialization and interpersonal effectiveness to emotional sensitivity. *Journal of Social Work Education, 21,* 74-84.

Janzen, C. (1978). Family therapy for alcoholism: A review. *Social Work, 23,* 135-141.

Jayaratne, S. (1977). Single-subject and group designs in treatment and evaluation. *Social Work Research & Abstracts, 13,* 35-42.

Jayaratne, S. (1978). A study of clinical eclecticism. *Social Service Review, 52,* 621-631.

Jayaratne, S. (1979). Analysis of selected social work journals and productivity ranking among schools of social work. *Journal of Education for Social Work, 15,* 72-80.

Jayaratne, S. (1982). Characteristics and theoretical orientations of clinical social workers: A national survey. *Journal of Social Service Research, 4,* 17-30.

Jayaratne, S., & Chess, W. A. (1983). Job satisfaction and burnout in social work. In B. A. Farber (Ed.), *Stress and burnout in the human service professions* (pp. 129-141). New York: Pergamon.

Jayaratne, S., & Chess, W. A. (1984). Job satisfaction, burnout and turnover: A national study. *Social Work, 29,* 448-453.

Jayaratne, S., & Chess, W. A. (1986). Job satisfaction: A comparison of caseworkers and administrators. *Social Work, 31,* 144-146.

Jayaratne, S., Chess, W. A., & Kunkel, D. A. (1986). Burnout: Its impact on child welfare workers and their spouses. *Social Work, 31,* 53-59.

Jayaratne, S., & Daniels, W. (1981). Measurement cross-validation using replication procedures within single-case designs. *Social Work Research & Abstracts, 17,* 4-10.

Jayaratne, S., & Ivey, K. V. (1981). Gender differences in the perceptions of social workers. *Social Casework, 62,* 405-412.

Jayaratne, S., & Levy, R. L. (1979). *Empirical clinical practice.* New York: Columbia University Press.

Jayaratne, S., Siefert, K., & Chess, W. A. (1988). Private and agency practitioners: Some data and observations. *Social Service Review, 62,* 324-336.

Jayaratne, S., Tripodi, T., & Chess, W. A. (1983). Perceptions of emotional support, stress and strain by male and female social workers. *Social Work Research & Abstracts, 19,* 19-27.

Jenkins, S. (1987). The limited domain of effectiveness research. *British Journal of Social Work, 17,* 587-593.

Jennings, P. L., & Dailey, M. (1979). Sex discrimination in social work careers. *Social Work Research & Abstracts, 15,* 17-21.

Johnson, H. C. (1986). Emerging concerns in family therapy. *Social Work, 31,* 299-306.

Johnson, M., & Stone, G. L. (1987). Social workers and burnout: A psychological description. *Journal of Social Service Research, 10,* 67-80.

Johnson, S. M., & Greenberg, L. S. (1985). Emotionally focused couples therapy: An outcome study. *Journal of Marital and Family Therapy, 11.*

Joseph, M. V., & Conrad, A. P. (1983). Teaching social work ethics for contemporary practice: An effectiveness evaluation. *Journal of Education for Social Work, 19,* 59-68.

Judah, E. H. (1979). Values: The uncertain component in social work. *Journal of Education for Social Work, 15,* 79-86.

Justice, B., & Justice, R. (1976). *The abusing family.* New York: Human Science Press.

Kadushin, A. (1974). Supervisor-supervisee: A survey. *Social Work, 19,* 288-297.

Kadushin, A. (1985). *Supervision in social work* (2nd ed.). New York: Columbia University Press.

Kadushin, A., & Kelling, G. (1977). An innovative program reducing length of training: Evaluation procedures and outcomes. *Journal of Education for Social Work, 13,* 68-75.

Kagle, J. D., & Cowger, C. D. (1984). Blaming the client: Implicit agenda in practice research? *Social Work, 29,* 347-351.

Kanter, J. S. (1983). Reevaluation of task-centered social work practice. *Clinical Social Work Journal, 11,* 228-244.

Kaplan, D. M. (1983). Current trends in practicum supervision research. *Counselor Education and Supervision, 22,* 215-226.

Karger, H. J. (1983). Science, research and social work: Who controls the profession? *Social Work, 28,* 200-205.

Kassel, S. L., & Kane, R. A. (1980). Self-determination dissected. *Clinical Social Work Journal, 8,* 161-178.

Kaul, T. J., & Bednar, R. L. (1986). Research in group and related therapies. In S. L. Garfield and A. E. Bergin (Eds.), *Handbook of psychotherapy and behavior change.* (3rd ed., pp. 671-714). New York: Wiley.

Kazdin, A. E. (1979). Data evaluation for intra-subject replication research. *Journal of Social Service Research, 3,* 79-97.

Keefe, T. (1975). Empathy and social work education: A study. *Journal of Education for Social Work, 11,* 69-75.

Keefe, T. (1979). The development of empathic skill: A study. *Journal of Education for Social Work, 15,* 30-37.

Kenmore, T. K. (1987). Negotiating with clients: A study of clinical practice experience. *Social Service Review, 61,* 132-143.

Kermish, I., & Kushin, F. (1969). Why high turnover? Social work staff losses in a county welfare department. *Public Welfare, 27,* 134-139.

Kiesler, D. J. (1971). Experimental designs in psychotherapy research. In A. E. Bergin & S. L. Garfield (Eds.), *Handbook of psychotherapy and behavior change.* New York: Wiley.

Killian, E. C. (1970). Effect of geriatric transfer on mortality rates. *Social Work, 15,* 19-26.

Kiresuk, T., & Sherman, R. (1968). Goal-Attainment Scaling: A general method for evaluating community mental health programs. *Community Mental Health Journal, 4,* 443-453.

Kirk, S. A., & Fischer, J. (1976). Do social workers understand research? *Journal of Education for Social Work, 12,* 63-70.

Kirk, S. A., Osmalov, M. J., & Fischer, J. (1976). Social workers' involvement in research. *Social Work, 21,* 121-124.

Kirk, S. A., Siporin, M., & Kutchins, H. (1989). The prognosis for social work diagnosis. *Social Casework, 70,* 295-304.

Knapman, S. K. (1977). Sex discrimination in family agencies. *Social Work, 22,* 461-465.

Koeske, G. F., & Crouse, M. A. (1981). Liberalism-conservatism in samples of social work students and professionals. *Social Service Review, 55,* 193-205.

Kolevzon, M. S., & Maykranz, J. (1982). Theoretical orientation and clinical practice: Uniformity versus eclecticism? *Social Service Review, 56,* 120-129.

Kopp, J. (1988). Self-monitoring: A literature review of research and practice. *Social Work Research & Abstracts, 24,* 8-20.

Kramer, H., Mathews, G., & Endias, R. (1987). Comparative stress levels in part-time and full-time social work programs. *Journal of Social Work Education, 23,* 74-80.

Kravetz, D., & Jones, L. E. (1982). Career orientations of female social work students: An examination of sex differences. *Journal of Education for Social Work, 18,* 77-84.

Kurtz, P. D., Marshall, E., & Holloway, R. (1982). Use of students to teach interviewing skills: An empirical evaluation. *Journal of Social Service Research, 6,* 63-78.

Kutchins, H., & Kirk, S. A. (1986). The reliability of DSM-III: A critical review. *Social Work Research & Abstracts, 22,* 3-12.

Kutchins, H., & Kirk, S. A. (1987). DSM-III and social work malpractice. *Social Work, 32,* 205-211.

Kutchins, H., & Kirk, S. A. (1989). DSM-III-R: The conflict over new psychiatric diagnoses. *Health and Social Work, 14,* 91-101.

Lambert, M. J., Asay, T. P. (1984). Patient characteristics and their relationship to psychotherapy outcome. In M. Hersen, L. Michelson, & A. S. Bellack (Eds.), *Issues in psychotherapy research* (pp. 313-359). New York: Plenum.

Lambert, M. J., Shapiro, D. A., & Bergin, A. E. (1986). The effectiveness of psychotherapy. In S. L. Garfield & A. E. Bergin (Eds.), *Psychotherapy and behavior change* (3rd ed., pp. 157-211). New York: Wiley.

Lang, N. C. (1979). A comparative examination of therapeutic uses of groups in social work and in adjacent human service professions: Part II. The literature from 1969-1978. *Social Work with Groups, 2,* 197-220.

Larsen, D. L., Attkisson, C. C., Hargreaves, W. A., & Nguyen, T. D. (1979). Assessment of client/patient satisfaction: Development of a general scale. *Evaluation and Program Planning, 2,* 197-207.

Larsen, J., & Hepworth, D. H. (1978). Skill development through competency-based education. *Journal of Education for Social Work, 14,* 73-81.

Latting, J. E., & Zundel, C. (1986). World view differences between clients and counselors. *Social Casework, 67,* 533-541.

Lawrence, H., & Walter, C. L. (1978). Testing a behavioral approach with groups. *Social Work, 23,* 127-133.

LeCroy, C. W. (1982). Practitioner competence in social work: Training and evaluation. *Journal of Social Service Research, 5,* 71-83.

LeCroy, C. W., & Rank, M. R. (1987). Factors associated with burnout in the social services: An exploratory study. *Journal of Social Service Research, 10,* 23-39.

Levinson, H. M. (1973). Use and misuse of groups. *Social Work, 18,* 66-73.

Levitt, J., & Reid, W. J. (1982). Rapid assessment instruments for practice. *Social Work Research & Abstracts, 17,* 13-20.

Levy, R. L. (1987). Treatment compliance in social work. *Journal of Social Service Research, 10,* 85-103.

Levy, R. L., & Olson, D. G. (1979). The single-subject methodology in clinical practice: An overview. *Journal of Social Service Research, 3,* 25-49.

Liberman, M. A. (1986). Social supports—the consequences of psychologizing: A commentary. *Journal of Consulting and Clinical Psychology, 54,* 461-465.

Lima, K. R., Eisenthal, S., & Lazare, A. (1982). Perception of requests in psychotherapy: Patient and therapist. *Journal of Social Service Research, 4,* 51-68.

Lindenberg, R. E., & Coulton, C. (1980). Planning for posthospital care: A follow-up study. *Health and Social Work, 5,* 45-50.

Lindsey, E. W., Yarbrough, D. B., & Morton, T. D. (1981). Evaluating interpersonal skills training for public welfare staff. *Social Service Review, 55,* 623-635.

Linn, M. W, & Greenwald, S. R. (1974). Student attitudes, knowledge and skill related to research training. *Journal of Education for Social Work, 10,* 48-54.

Linsk, N., Howe, M. W., & Pinkston, E. M. (1975). Behavioral group work in a home for the aged. *Social Work, 20,* 454-463.

Lister, L. (1980). Role expectations of social workers and other health professionals. *Health and Social Work, 5,* 41-49.

Locker, D., & Dunt, D. (1978). Theoretical and methodological issues in sociological studies of consumer satisfaction with medical care. *Social Science & Medicine, 12,* 283-292.

Lowy, L. (1983). Social work supervision: From models toward theory. *Journal of Education for Social Work, 19,* 55-62.

Ludwig, E. G., & Gibson, G. (1969). Self-perception of sickness and the seeking of medical care. *Journal of Health and Social Behavior, 10,* 125-133.

Lurie, A. (1979). Clinical social work contribution to social work. In P. L. Ewalt (Ed.), *Toward a definition of clinical social work* (pp. 75-86). Washington, DC: NASW.

Maas, H. S. (1966). *Five fields of social service: Reviews of research.* New York: NASW.

Maas, H. S. (1971). *Research in the social services: A five-year review.* New York: NASW.

Mackey, R. A., Burdek, M., & Charkoudion, S. (1987). The relationship of theory to clinical practice. *Clinical Social Work Journal, 15,* 368-383.

Magura, S. (1982). Clients view outcomes of child protective services. *Social Casework, 62,* 522-531.

Maluccio, A. N. (1979). Perspectives of social workers and clients on treatment outcome. *Social Casework, 60,* 394-401.

Marecek, J., & Johnson, M. (1980). Gender and the process of therapy. In A. M. Brodsky & R. L. Hare-Mustin (Eds.), *Women and psychotherapy: An assessment of research and practice* (pp. 67-93). New York: Guilford.

Marsh, J. C. (1980). Help seeking among addicted and nonaddicted women of low socioeconomic status. *Social Service Review, 54,* 239-248.

Marsh, J. C. (1983). Research and innovation in social work practice: Avoiding the headless machine. *Social Service Review, 57,* 582-598.

Marsh, S. R. (1988). Antecedents to choice of a helping career: Social work vs. business majors. *Smith College Studies in Social Work, 58,* 85-100.

Marshall, E. K., Charping, J. W., & Bell, W. J. (1979). Interpersonal skills training: A review of the research. *Social Work Research & Abstracts, 15,* 10-16.

Marshall, E. K., & Mazie, A. S. (1987). A cognitive approach to treating depression. *Social Casework, 68,* 540-545.

Marziali, E. (1988). The first session: An interpersonal encounter. *Social Casework, 69,* 23-27.

Masek, B. J. (1982). Compliance and medicine. In D. M. Doleys, R. L. Meredith, & A. R. Ciminero (Eds.), *Behavioral medicine: Assessment and treatment strategies.* New York: Plenum.

Maslach, C. (1982). *Burnout: The cost of caring.* Englewood Cliffs, NJ: Prentice-Hall.

Maslach, C. (1987). Burnout research in the social services: A critique. *Journal of Social Service Research, 10,* 95-105.

Maslach, C., & Jackson, S. E. (1981). *Maslach burnout inventory.* Palo Alto, CA: Consulting Psychologists Press.

Matarazzo, R. G. (1978). Research in the teaching and learning of psychotherapeutic skills. In S. Garfield & A. Bergin (Eds.), *A handbook of psychotherapy and behavior change* (2nd ed., pp. 941-966). New York: Wiley.

Matarazzo, R. G., & Patterson, D. R. (1986). Methods of teaching therapeutic skill. In S. L. Garfield & A. E. Bergin (Eds.), *Handbook of psychotherapy and behavior change* (3rd ed., pp. 821-843). New York: Wiley.

Mayadas, N. S., & Duehn, W. D. (1977). The effects of training formats and interpersonal discriminations in the education for clinical social work practice. *Journal of Social Service Research, 1,* 147-161.

Mayer, J. E., & Rubin, G. (1983). Is there a future for social work in HMOs? *Health and Social Work, 8,* 283-289.

Mayer, J. E., & Timms, N. (1969). Clash in perspective between worker and client. *Social Casework, 50,* 32-40.

McCreath, J. (1984). The new generation of chronic psychiatric patients. *Social Work, 29,* 436-441.

McIntyre, E. L. G. (1986). Social networks: Potential for practice. *Social Work, 31,* 421-426.

McNeece, C. A. (1981). Faculty publications, tenure and job satisfaction in graduate social work programs. *Journal of Education for Social Work, 17,* 13-19.

Meichenbaum, D., & Turk, D. C. (1987). *Facilitating treatment adherence: A practitioner's guidebook.* New York: Plenum.

Merdinger, J. M. (1982). Socialization into a profession: The case of undergraduate social work students. *Journal of Education for Social Work, 18,* 12-19.

Miller, R. S., & Rehr, M. (1983). *Social work issues in health care.* Englewood Cliffs, NJ: Prentice-Hall.

Mor, V., & Laliberte, L. (1984). Burnout among hospice staff. *Health and Social Work, 9,* 274-283.

Most, E. (1964). Measuring change in marital satisfaction. *Social Work, 9,* 64-70.

Mullen, E. J., Chazin, R. M., & Feldstein, D. M. (1972). Services for the newly dependent: An assessment. *Social Service Review, 46,* 309-322.

Munson, C. E. (1979). Evaluation of male and female supervisors. *Social Work, 24,* 104-110.

Munson, C. E. (1981). Style and structure in supervision. *Journal of Education for Social Work, 17,* 65-72.

Munson, C. E. (1983). *An introduction to clinical social work supervision.* New York: Haworth Press.

Murch, M. (1980). *Justice and welfare in divorce.* London: Sweet and Maxwell.

Mutschler, E. (1979). Using single-case evaluation procedures in family and children's service agency: Integration of practice and research. *Journal of Social Service Research, 3,* 115-134.

Mutschler, E. (1984). Evaluating practice: A study of research utilization by practitioners. *Social Work, 29,* 332-337.

Mutschler, E., & Rosen, A. (1977). Influence of content relevant and irrelevant client verbalizations on interviewer affect. *Journal of Social Service Research, 1,* 51-61.

Mutschler, E., & Rosen, A. (1979). Evaluation of treatment outcome by client and social worker. *Social Welfare Forum, 109,* 156-165.

Nelsen, J. C. (1985). Verifying the independent variable in single-subject research. *Social Work Research & Abstracts, 21,* 3-8.

Nuehring, E. M., & Ladner, R. A. (1980). Use of aftercare programs in community mental health clinics. *Social Work Research & Abstracts, 16,* 34-40.

Nuehring, E. M., & Pascone, A. B. (1986). Single-subject evaluation: A tool for quality assurance. *Social Work, 31,* 359-365.

Nugent, W. R. (1987). Information gain through integrated research approaches. *Social Service Review, 61,* 337-364.

Nurius, P. S., & Tripodi, T. (1985). Methods of generalization used in empirical social work literature. *Social Service Review, 59,* 239-257.

Nurius, P. S., Wedenoja, M., & Tripodi, T. (1987). Prescriptions, proscriptions and generalization in social work direct practice literature. *Social Casework, 68,* 589-596.

O'Connor, I., & Dalgleish, L. (1986). The impact of social work education: A personal construct reconceptualization. *Journal of Social Work Education, 22,* 6-21.

O'Connor, R., & Reid, W. J. (1986). Dissatisfaction with brief treatment. *Social Service Review, 60,* 526-537.

O'Neil, M. J. (1980). A comparative study of social workers from one- and two-year graduate social work programs. *Journal of Education for Social Work, 16,* 75-81.

Orlinsky, D. E., & Howard, K. E. (1978). The relation of process to outcome of psychotherapy. In S. L. Garfield & A. E. Bergin (Eds.), *Handbook of psychotherapy and behavior change: An empirical analysis* (2nd ed., pp. 283-329). New York: Wiley.

Orlinsky, D. E., & Howard, K. I. (1986). Process and outcome in psychotherapy. In S. L. Garfield & A. E. Bergin (Eds.), *Handbook of psychotherapy and behavior change* (3rd ed., pp. 311-381). New York: Wiley.

Orme, J. G., & Gillespie, D. F. (1986). Reliability and bias in categorizing individual client problems. *Social Service Review, 60,* 161-174.

Orme, J. G., Gillespie, D. F., & Fortune, A. E. (1983). Two dimensional summary scores derived from ratings of individualized client problems. *Social Work Research & Abstracts, 18,* 30-32.

Orten, J. D. (1981). Influencing attitudes: A study of social work students. *Social Work Research & Abstracts, 17,* 11-17.

Pahl, J. (1985). *Private violence and public policy.* London: Routledge and Kegan Paul.

Palmer, T. B. (1973). Matching worker and client in corrections. *Social Work, 18,* 95-103.

Paquet-Deehy, A., Hopmeyer, E., Home, A., & Kislowicz, L. (1985). A typology of social work practice with groups. *Social Work with Groups, 8,* 65-78.

Parry, J. K., & Smith, M. J. (1988). A study of social workers' job satisfaction as based on an optimal model of care for the terminally ill. *Journal of Social Service Research, 11,* 39-58.

Patchner, M. A., & Wattenberg, S. H. (1985). Impact of diagnostic related groups on hospital social service departments. *Social Work, 30,* 259-261.

Peile, C. (1988). Research paradigms in social work: From stalemate to creative synthesis. *Social Service Review, 62*, 1-19.

Petchers, M. K., & Milligan, S. E. (1987). Social networks and social support among black urban elderly: A health care resource. *Social Work in Health Care, 12*, 103-117.

Peterson, K. J., & Anderson, S. C. (1984). Evaluation of social work practice in health care settings. *Social Work in Health Care, 10*, 1-16.

Petty, M. M., & Odewahn, C. A. (1983). Supervisory behavior and sex role stereotypes in human service organizations. *The Clinical Supervisor, 12*, 13-20.

Pfouts, J. H., & Henley, H. C. (1977). Admissions roulette: Predictive factors for success in practice. *Journal of Education for Social Work, 13*, 56-62.

Pfouts, J. H., & McDaniels, B. (1977). Medical handmaidens or professional colleagues: A survey of social work practice in the pediatrics departments of twenty-eight teaching hospitals. *Social Work in Health Care, 2*, 275-283.

Phares, J. E. (1976). *Locus of control in personality.* New Jersey: General Learning Press.

Pharis, M. E., & Williams, B. E. (1984). Further developments in societies for clinical social work: A ten-year follow-up study. *Clinical Social Work Journal, 12*, 164-178.

Phillips, D. L. (1965). Self-reliance and the inclination to adopt the sick role. *Social Forces, 43*, 555-563.

Phillips, L. E. (1985). *Psychotherapy revisited: New frontiers in research and practice.* Hillsdale, NJ: Lawrence Erlbaum Associates.

Phillips, W. R. (1977). Attitudes toward social work in family medicine: A before and after survey. *Social Work in Health Care, 3*, 61-66.

Pieper, M. H. (1985). The future of social work research. *Social Work Research & Abstracts, 21*, 3-11.

Pines, A., & Kafry, D. (1978). Occupational tedium in the social services. *Social Work, 23*, 499-507.

Platman, S. (1983). Family caretaking and expressed emotions: An evaluation. *Hospital and Community Psychiatry, 34*, 923.

Plotnick, H. L. (1977). Factors affecting student accuracy in predicting client behavior. *Journal of Education for Social Work, 13*, 91-98.

Poertner, J., & Rapp, C. A. (1983). What is social work supervision? *The Clinical Supervisor, 1*, 53-65.

Poole, D. L., & Braja, L. J. (1984). Does social work in HMOs measure up to professional standards? *Health and Social Work, 9*, 305-313.

Pratt, L. (1970). Optimism-pessimism about helping the poor with health problems. *Social Work, 15*, 29-33.

Presley, J. H. (1987). The clinical dropout: A view from the client's perspective. *Social Casework, 68*, 603-608.

Proctor, E. K. (1983). Variables in the structuring of early treatment. *Social Work Research & Abstracts, 19*, 26-33.

Proctor, E. K., & Rosen, A. (1983). Problem formulation and its relation to treatment planning. *Social Work Research & Abstracts, 19*, 22-27.

Radin, N., Benbenishty, R., & Leon, J. (1982). Predictors of success in a social work doctoral program. *Social Service Review, 56*, 640-658.

Ramsey, P. C. (1989). Practice orientations of students in field instruction. *The Clinical Supervisor, 7*, 137-160.

Raskin, M. S. (1982). Factors associated with student satisfaction in undergraduate social work field placements, *Arete, 7*, 44-54.

Ratliff, N. (1988). Stress and burnout in the helping professions. *Social Casework, 69,* 147-154.

Reamer, F. G. (1985). Facing up to the challenge of DRGs. *Health and Social Work, 10,* 85-94.

Reardon, G. T., Blumenfield, S., Weissman, A. L., & Rosenberg, G. (1988). Findings and implications from preadmission screening of elderly patients waiting for elective surgery. *Social Work in Health Care, 13,* 51-63.

Rehr, H. (1983). The consumer and consumerism. In R. S. Miller & H. Rehr (Eds.), *Social work issues in health care* (pp. 20-73). Englewood Cliffs, NJ: Prentice-Hall.

Rehr, H. (1984). Health care and social work services: Present concerns and future directions. *Social Work in Health Care, 10,* 71-83.

Rehr, H., Berkman, B., & Rosenberg, G. (1980). Screening for high social risk: Principles and problems. *Social Work, 25,* 403-406.

Reid, P. N., & Gundlach, J. H. (1983). A scale for the measurement of consumer satisfaction with social services. *Journal of Social Service Research, 7,* 37-54.

Reid, W. J. (1967). Characteristics of casework intervention. *Welfare in Review, 5,* 11-19.

Reid, W. J. (1974). Developments in the use of organized data. *Social Work, 19,* 585-593.

Reid, W. J. (1975). A test of a task-centered approach. *Social Work, 20,* 3-9.

Reid, W. J. (1978). *The task-centered system.* New York: Columbia University Press.

Reid, W. J. (1984). Treatment of choice or choice of treatments: An essay review. *Social Work Research & Abstracts, 20,* 33-37.

Reid, W. J. (1987). Evaluating an intervention in developmental research. *Journal of Social Service Research, 11,* 17-37.

Reid, W. J., & Beard, C. (1980). An evaluation of in-service training in a public welfare setting. *Administration in Social Work, 4,* 71-85.

Reid, W. J., & Epstein, L. (1972). *Task-centered casework.* New York: Columbia University Press.

Reid, W. J., & Epstein, L. (1977). *Task-centered practice.* New York: Columbia University Press.

Reid, W. J., & Hanrahan, P. (1982). Recent evaluations of social work: Grounds for optimism. *Social Work, 27,* 328-340.

Reid, W. J., & Shyne, A. W. (1969). *Brief and extended casework.* New York: Columbia University Press.

Reinherz, H., Grob, M. C., & Berkman, B. (1983). Health agencies and a school of social work: Practice and research in partnership. *Health & Social Work, 8,* 40-47.

Reiter, L. (1980). Professional morale and social work training: A study. *Clinical Social Work Journal, 8,* 198-205.

Resnick, G. (1985). The short and long-term impact of a competency-based program for disadvantaged women. *Journal of Social Service Research, 7,* 37-49.

Reynolds, M. K., & Cryms, J. T. (1970). A survey of the use of family therapy by caseworkers. *Social Casework, 51,* 76-81.

Rhodes, S. L. (1977). Contract negotiation in the initial stages of casework service. *Social Service Review, 51,* 125-140.

Richard, R. (1975). Non-users of medical facilities: The emergence of self-reliance. *Canadian Journal of Public Health, 66,* 477-480.

Richey, C. A., Blythe, B. J., & Berlin, S. B. (1987). Do social workers evaluate their practice? *Social Work Research & Abstracts, 23,* 14-20.

Richman, J. M., & Rosenfeld, L. B. (1988). Advanced standing versus regular two-year MSW graduates: Program evaluation and employment history. *Journal of Social Work Education, 24,* 13-19.

Rivas, R. F., & Toseland, R. (1981). The student group leadership evaluation project: A study of group leadership skills. *Social Work with Groups, 4,* 159-175.

Rock, B. D. (1987). Goal and outcome in social work practice. *Social Work, 33,* 393-398.

Rogers, C. R. (1957). The necessary and sufficient conditions of therapeutic personality change. *Journal of Consulting Psychology, 21,* 95-103.

Rohrbaugh, M. (1983). Schizophrenia research: Swimming against the mainstream. *Family Therapy Networker, 7,* 29-31, 61-52.

Rooney, R. H. (1985). Does inservice training make a difference? Results of a pilot study of task-centered dissemination in a public social service setting. *Journal of Social Service Research, 8,* 33-50.

Rose, S. D. (1978). The effect of contingency contracting on the completion rate of behavioral assignments in assertion training groups. *Journal of Social Service Research, 1,* 299-305.

Rose, S. D. (1981). How group attributes relate to outcome in behavior group therapy. *Social Work Research & Abstracts, 17,* 25-29.

Rose, S. D., & Edleson, J. F. (1979). Interpersonal skill training for social workers in small groups. *Social Work with Groups, 2,* 77-86.

Rosen, A. (1979). Evaluating doctoral programs in social work: A case study. *Social Work Research & Abstracts, 15,* 19-27.

Rosen, A. (1983). Barriers to utilization of research by social work practitioners. *Journal of Social Service Research, 6,* 1-15.

Rosen, A., & Cohen, M. (1980). Client expectation-preference discrepancies, perceived powerlessness and treatment behaviors. *Journal of Social Service Research, 3,* 371-381.

Rosen, A., & Liberman, D. (1972). The experimental evaluation of interview performance of social workers. *Social Service Review, 46,* 395-412.

Rosen, A., & Mutschler, E. (1982a). Correspondence between the planned and subsequent use of interventions in treatment. *Social Work Research & Abstracts, 18,* 28-34.

Rosen, A., & Proctor, E. K. (1979). Specifying the treatment process: The basis for effective research. *Journal of Social Service Research, 2,* 25-43.

Rosenblatt, A., & Kirk, S. A. (1981). Cumulative effect of research courses on knowledge and attitudes of social work students. *Journal of Education for Social Work, 17,* 26-34.

Rothman, B., & Fike, D. (1988). To seize the moment: Opportunities in the CSWE standards for group work research. *Social Work with Groups, 10,* 91-109.

Rotter, J. B. (1966). Generalized expectations for internal versus external control of reinforcement. *Psychological Monographs, 8,* (1, Whole No. 609).

Rubenstein, H., & Bloch, M. H. (1978). Helping clients who are poor: Worker and client perceptions of problems, activities and outcomes. *Social Service Review, 52,* 69-84.

Rubin, A. (1981). Reexamining the impact of sex on salary: The limits of statistical significance. *Social Work Research & Abstracts, 17,* 19-24.

Rubin, A. (1982). Why do women occupy lower academic ranks: Discrimination or progress? *Social Work Research & Abstracts, 18,* 19-23.

Rubin, A. (1984). Community-based care of the mentally ill: A research review. *Health & Social Work, 9,* 165-177.

Rubin, A. (1985). Practice effectiveness: More grounds for optimism. *Social Work, 30,* 469-476.

Rubin, A., & Babbie, E. (1989). *Research methods for social work.* Belmont, CA: Woodsworth.

Rubin, A., & Johnson, P. J. (1984). Direct practice interests of entering MSW students. *Journal of Education for Social Work, 20,* 5-16.

Rubin, A., Johnson, P. J., & DeWeaver, K. L. (1986). Direct practice interests of MSW students: Changes from entry to graduation. *Journal of Social Work Education, 22,* 98-108.

Ruckdeschel, R. A. (1985). Qualitative research as a perspective. *Social Work Research & Abstracts, 21,* 17-21.

Ruckdeschel, R., & Farris, B. (1981). Assessing practice: A critical look at single-case design. *Social Casework, 62,* 413-419.

Russell, M. N. (1984). *Skills in counseling women: The feminist approach.* Springfield, IL: C. C. Thomas.

Russell, M. N., James, R., & Berlow, J. (1987). Preventing discontinuity in community care of arthritis patients: A follow-up study of transfer. *Canadian Journal of Public Health, 78,* 119-123.

Russell, M. N., Lang, M., & Brett, B. (1987). Reducing dropout rates through improved intake procedures. *Social Casework, 68,* 421-425.

Russell, M. N., Lipov, E., Phillips, N., & White, B. (1989). Psychological profiles of violent and nonviolent maritally distressed couples. *Psychotherapy, 26,* 81-87.

Russell, P. A., Lankford, M. W., & Grinnell, R. M. (1983). Attitudes toward supervisors in a human service agency. *The Clinical Supervisor, 1,* 57-71.

Rutholz, T., & Werk, A. (1984). Student supervision: An educational process. *The Clinical Supervisor, 2,* 15-27.

Saari, C. (1987). *Clinical social work treatment: How does it work?* New York: Gardner.

Sainsbury, E. (1987). Client studies: Their contributions and limitations in influencing social work practice. *British Journal of Social Work, 17,* 635-644.

Sainsbury, E., Nixon, S., & Phillips, D. (1982). *Social work in focus.* London: Routledge and Kegan Paul.

Saleeby, D. (1979). The tension between research and practice: The assumptions of the experimental paradigm. *Clinical Social Work Journal, 7,* 267-284.

Schilit, R., & Gomberg, E. L. (1987). Social support structures of women in treatment for alcoholism. *Health and Social Work, 12,* 187-195.

Schilling, R. F., II. (1987). Limitations of social support. *Social Service Review, 61,* 19-31.

Schinke, S. P. (1979). Evaluating social work practice: A conceptual model and example. *Social Casework, 60,* 195-200.

Schinke, S. P., Blythe, B. J., Gilchrist, L. D., & Smith, T. E. (1980). Developing intake-interviewing skills. *Social Work Research & Abstracts, 16,* 29-34.

Schinke, S. P., Smith, T. E., Gilchrist, L. D., & Wong, S. E. (1978). Interviewing-skills training: An empirical evaluation. *Journal of Social Service Research, 1,* 391-401.

Schlessinger, E. G., & Wolock, I. (1974). An accelerated and traditional MSW program compared. *Journal of Education for Social Work, 10,* 68-76.

Schofield, W. (1964). *Psychotherapy. The purchase of friendship.* Englewood Cliffs, NJ: Prentice-Hall.

Schuerman, J. R. (1975). Do family services help? An essay review. *Social Service Review, 49,* 363-375.

Schuerman, J. R. (1987). Passion, analysis and technology: The Social Service Review lecture. *Social Service Review, 61,* 3-18.

Scully, R. (1983). The work-setting support groups: A means of preventing burnout. In B. A. Farber (Ed.), *Stress and burnout in the human service professions* (pp. 188-197). New York: Pergamon.

Seaberg, J. R. (1970). Systematized recording: A follow-up. *Social Casework, 15,* 32-41.

Seaberg, J. R. (1981). IPR-2: A revised measure of outcome. *Social Work Research & Abstracts, 16,* 45-46.

Segal, A. (1970). Workers' perceptions of mentally disabled clients: Effect on service delivery. *Social Work, 15,* 39-46.

Segal, S. P. (1972). Research on the outcome of social work therapeutic interventions: A review of the literature. *Journal of Health & Social Behavior, 13,* 3-17.

Selig, A. L. (1978). Evaluating a social work department in a psychiatric hospital. *Health and Social Work, 3,* 72-87.

Selig, A. L. (1980). Those back in one year: A study of readmissions to a university health sciences centre psychiatric hospital. *Journal of Social Service Research, 3,* 267-281.

Selig, A. L., Reber, P., Phanidis, J., & Roberston, G. (1982). Social workers as evaluators: A case study of a program for consumer feedback in a psychiatric hospital. *Social Work in Health Care, 7,* 67-78.

Shapiro, C. H., Mueller-Lazar, B. J., & Witkin, S. L. (1980). Performance-based evaluation: A diagnostic tool for educators. *Social Service Review, 54,* 262-272.

Sharwell, G. R. (1974). Can values be taught? A study of two variables related to orientation of social work graduate students toward public dependency. *Journal of Education for Social Work, 10,* 99-105.

Shatkin, B. F., Frisman, L. K., & McGuire, T. G. (1986). The effect of vendorship on the distribution of clinical social work services. *Social Service Review, 60,* 437-448.

Sheldon, B. (1987). Implementing findings from social work effectiveness research. *British Journal of Social Work, 17,* 573-586.

Shinn, M. (1982). Methodological issues: Evaluating and using information. In W. S. Paine (Ed.), *Job stress and burnout: Research, theory and intervention perspectives* (pp. 61-79). Beverly Hills, CA: Sage.

Shulman, L. (1978). A study of practice skills. *Social Work, 23,* 274-280.

Shulman, L. (1981). *Identifying, measuring and teaching helping skills.* New York: NASW.

Shulman, L., Robinson, E., & Luckyj, A. (1981). *A study of the content, context and skills of supervision.* Vancouver: University of British Columbia Report.

Siegel, D. H. (1983). Can research and practice be integrated in social work education? *Journal of Education for Social Work, 19,* 12-19.

Siegel, D. H. (1985). Effective teaching of empirically based practice. *Social Work Research & Abstracts, 21,* 40-48.

Silverman, M. (1966). Knowledge in social group work: A review of the literature. *Social Work, 11,* 56-62.

Simons, R. L. (1984). Practice implications of outcome research. *Social Work, 29,* 401-403.

Simons, R. L. (1987). The impact of training for empirically based practice. *Journal of Social Work Education, 23,* 24-30.

Sinclair, I., & Walker, D. (1985). Task-centered casework in two intake teams. In E. M. Goldberg, J. Gibbons, & I. Sinclair (Eds.), *Problems, tasks and outcomes: The evaluation of task-centered casework in three settings* (pp. 13-85). London: Allen & Unwin.

Singh, R. M. (1982). Brief interviews: Approaches, techniques and effectiveness. *Social Casework, 63,* 599-606.

Siporin, M. (1983). The therapeutic process in clinical social work. *Social Work, 28,* 193-198.

Siporin, M. (1985). Current social work perspectives on clinical practice. *Clinical Social Work Journal, 13,* 198-217.

Sirles, E. A. (1982). Client-counselor agreement on problem and change. *Social Casework, 62,* 248-253.

Smith, C. J., & Smith, C. A. (1979). Evaluating outcome measures for deinstitutionalization progress. *Social Work Research & Abstracts, 15,* 23-30.

Smith, D. (1987). The limits of positivism in social work research. *British Journal of Social Work, 17,* 401-416.

Smith, S. L., & Baker, D. R. (1989). The relationship between educational background of field instructors and the quality of supervision. *The Clinical Supervisor, 7,* 257-270.

Snyder, D. K., & Wills, R. M. (1989). Behavioral versus insight-oriented marital therapy: Effects on individual and interspousal functioning. *Journal of Consulting and Clinical Psychology, 57,* 39-46.

Solomon, P., & Davis, J. M. (1986). The effects of alcohol abuse among the new chronically mentally ill. *Social Work in Health Care, 11,* 65-74.

Soroker, E. P. (1977). An analysis of pediatric outpatient care. *Health and Social Work, 2,* 89-103.

Sowers-Hoag, K., & Thyer, B. A. (1985). Teaching social work practice: A review and analysis of empirical research. *Journal of Social Work Education, 21,* 5-15.

Spano, R. M., Kiresuk, T. J., & Lund, S. H. (1978). An operational model to achieve accountability for social work in health care. *Social Work in Health Care, 3,* 123-141.

Specht, H. (1986). Social supports, social networks, social exchange, and social work practice. *Social Service Review, 60,* 218-240.

Specht, H., Britt, D., & Frost, C. (1984). Undergraduate education and profession achievement of MSWs. *Social Work, 29,* 219-224.

Specht, H., & Specht, R. (1986). Social work assessment: Route to clienthood-Part I. *Social Casework, 67,* 525-532.

Star, B. (1977). The effects of videotape self-image confrontation on helping perceptions. *Journal of Education for Social Work, 13,* 114-119.

Starr, R., & Walker, J. (1982). A comparison of part-time and full-time degree students: The one-year residence program advisors' study. *Journal of Education for Social Work, 18,* 59-67.

Stein, S., Linn, M. W., & Furdon, J. (1974). Predicting social work student performance. *Journal of Education for Social Work, 10,* 85-92.

Stockler, J. D., Sittler, R. & Davidson, G. E. (1966). Social work in a medical clinic: The nature and course of referrals to social work. *American Journal of Public Health, 56,* 1570-1579.

Stoller, E. P. (1982). Sources of support for the elderly during illness. *Health and Social Work, 7,* 111-122.

Stoltenberg, C. D., Pierce, R. A., & McNeill, B. W. (1987). Effects of experience on counselor trainees' needs. *The Clinical Supervisor, 5,* 23-32.

Streepy, J. (1981). Direct-service providers and burnout. *Social Casework, 62,* 353-361.

Strupp, H. (1978). Psychotherapy research & practice: An overview. In S. L. Garfield & A. E. Bergin (Eds.), *Handbook of psychotherapy and behavior change: An empirical analysis* (2nd ed., pp. 3-22). New York: Wiley.

Subramanian, K., & Rose, S. D. (1985). A group approach to the management of chronic pain. *Social Work Research & Abstracts, 21,* 29-30.

Subramanian, K., & Rose, S. D. (1988). Pain management treatment: A 2-year follow-up study. *Social Work, 33,* 2-3.

Sucato, V. (1978). The problem-solving process in short-term and long-term service. *Social Service Review, 52,* 244-262.

Sze, W. D., & Ivker, B. (1986). Stress in social workers: The impact of setting and role. *Social Casework, 67,* 141-148.

Sze, W. D., Kella, R., & Kella, D. B. (1979). A comparative study of two different teaching and curricular arrangements in human behavior and social environment. *Journal of Education for Social Work, 15*, 103-109.

Taggart, S. R. (1982). The baccalaureate social worker in the health care system. *Health and Social Work, 7*, 262-267.

Task Force on Quality in Graduate Social Work Education. (1986). The pursuit of excellence in social work education. *Journal of Social Work Education, 21*, 5-15.

Taubman, S. B. (1978). Isolating videotape training effects. *Journal of Social Service Research, 1*, 307-315.

Thomas, E. J. (1977). The BESDAS model for effective practice. *Social Work Research & Abstracts, 13*, 12-16.

Thomas, E. J. (1978). Research and service in single-case experimentation: Conflicts and choices. *Social Work Research & Abstracts, 44*, 20-31.

Thomas, E. J., Santa, C., Bronson, D., & Oyserman, D. (1987). Unilateral family therapy with the spouses of alcoholics. *Journal of Social Service Research, 10*, 145-162.

Thomlison, R. J. (1981). Outcome effectiveness research and its implications for social work educators. *Canadian Journal of Social Work Education, 1*, 55-91.

Thomlison, R. J. (1984). Something works: Evidence from practice effectiveness studies. *Social Work, 29*, 51-56.

Thyer, B. A., & Bentley, K. J. (1986). Academic affiliations of social work authors: A citation analysis of six major journals. *Journal of Social Work Education, 22*, 67-73.

Thyer, B. A., & Hudson, W. W. (1987). Progress in behavioral social work: An introduction. *Journal of Social Service Research, 10*, 7-35.

Thyer, B. A., Sowers-Hoag, K., & Love, J. P. (1986). The influence of field instructor-student gender combinations on student perceptions of field instruction quality. *Arete, 11*, 25-29.

Thyer, B. A., Williams, M., Love, J. P., & Sowers-Hoag, K. M. (1989). The MSW supervisory requirement in field instruction: Does it make a difference? *The Clinical Supervisor, 7*, 249-256.

Tolson, E. R., & Brown, L. B. (1981). Client dropout rate and students' practice skills in task-centered casework. *Social Casework, 62*, 308-313.

Tolson, E. R., & Kopp, J. (1988). The practicum: Clients, problems, interventions and influences on student practice. *Journal of Social Work Education, 24*, 123-134.

Torre, E. (1974). Student performance in solving social work problems and work experience prior to entering the MSW program. *Journal of Education for Social Work, 10*, 114-117.

Toseland, R. W. (1987). Treatment discontinuance: Grounds for optimism. *Social Casework, 68*, 195-203.

Toseland, R. W., Kohut, D., & Kemp, K. (1983). Evaluation of a smoking-cessation group treatment program. *Social Work Research & Abstracts, 19*, 12-19.

Toseland, R. W., Palmer-Ganeles, J., & Chapman, D. (1986). Teamwork in psychiatric settings. *Social Work, 31*, 46-52.

Toseland, R. W., & Reid, W. J. (1985). Using rapid assessment instruments in a family service agency. *Social Casework, 66*, 547-555.

Toseland, R., & Rose, S. D. (1978). Evaluating social skills training for older adults in groups. *Social Work Research & Abstracts, 14*, 25-33.

Toseland, R., Sherman, E., & Bliven, S. (1981). The comparative effectiveness of two group work approaches for the development of mutual support groups among the elderly. *Social Work with Groups, 4*, 137-153.

Toseland, R., & Spielberg, G. (1982). The development of helping skills in undergraduate social work education: Model and evaluation. *Journal of Education for Social Work, 18,* 66-73.

Tripodi, T., & Epstein, I. (1978). Incorporating knowledge of research methodology into social work practice. *Journal of Social Service Research, 2,* 65-78.

Truax, C. B., & Carkhuff, R. (1967). *Toward effective counseling and psychotherapy: Training and Practice.* Chicago: Aldine.

Turner, F. J. (1970). Ethnic differences and client performance. *Social Service Review, 44,* 1-10.

Ullman, A., Goss, M. E., Davis, M. S., & Mushinski, M. (1971). Activities, satisfaction and problems in social workers in hospital settings. *Social Service Review, 45,* 17-29.

Ullman, A., & Kassebaum, G. G. (1961). Referrals and services in a medical social work department. *Social Service Review, 35,* 258-267.

Varley, B. K. (1963). Socialization in social work education. *Social Work, 8,* 102-109.

Varley, B. K. (1968). Social work values. Changes in value commitments of students from admission to MSW graduation. *Journal of Education for Social Work, 4,* 67-76.

Viccaro, T. J. (1978). Social work practice with groups: A laboratory program for the beginning undergraduate students. *Social Work with Groups, 1,* 195-206.

Vigilante, F. W. (1983). Students' narcissism and academic performance. *Social Casework, 64,* 602-608.

Wallace, M. E. (1982). Private practice: A nationwide study. *Social Work, 27,* 262-267.

Walsh, S. F. (1986). Characteristics of failures in an emergency residential alternative to psychiatric hospitalization. *Social Work in Health Care, 11,* 56-63.

Ware, J. E., Snyder, M. K., Wright, W. R., & Davies, A. R. (1983). Defining and measuring patient satisfaction with medical care. *Evaluation and Program Planning, 6,* 247-263.

Wasserman, H. (1970). Early careers of professional social workers in public welfare agency. *Social Work, 15,* 93-101.

Watson, K. W. (1973). Differential supervision. *Social Work, 18,* 80-88.

Wattenberg, S. H., & O'Rourke, T. W. (1978). Comparison of task performance of master's and bachelor's degree social workers in hospitals. *Social Work in Health Care, 4,* 93-103.

Webb, A. P. & Riley, P. (1970). Effectiveness of casework with young female probationers. *Social Casework, 51,* 566-572.

Weed, L. L. (1969). *Medical records, medical education and patient care: The Problem-Oriented Record as a basic tool.* Chicago: The Press of Case Western Reserve University.

Weeks, W., Kotsubo, M., Kamishita, C., Yokoyama, M., Cross, L., & Fischer, J. (1977). Perceptions of empathy: A comparative study of caseworker, client and peer perceptions. *Canadian Journal of Social Work Education, 3,* 17-23.

Weissman, M. (1980). Depression. In A. M. Brodsky & R. T. Hare-Mustin (Eds.), *Women and psychotherapy: An assessment of research and practice* (pp. 97-112). New York: Guilford.

Welch, G. J. (1983). Will graduates use single-case design to evaluate their casework practice? *Journal of Education for Social Work, 19,* 42-47.

Wells, R. A., Figurel, J. A., & McNamee, P. (1977). Communication training vs. conjoint marital therapy. *Social Work Research & Abstracts, 13,* 31-39.

Werner, H. D. (1976). Casework can be effective. In J. Fischer (Ed.), *The effectiveness of social casework* (pp. 300-307). Springfield, IL: C. C. Thomas.

Wilks, R. J., & McCarthy, C. R. (1986). Intervention in child sexual abuse: A survey of attitudes. *Social Casework, 67,* 20-26.

Williams, H., Ho, L., & Fielder, L. (1974). Career patterns: More grist for women's liberation. *Social Work, 19,* 463-466.

Wilner, D. M., Freeman, H. E., Surber, M., & Goldstein, M. S. (1985). Success in mental health treatment interventions: A review of 211 random assignment studies. *Journal of Social Service Research, 8,* 1-20.

Witkin, S. L. (1989). Toward a scientific social work. *Journal of Social Service Research, 12,* 83-98.

Witkin, S. L., & Harrison, D. F. (1979). Single-case design in marital research and therapy. *Journal of Social Service Research, 3,* 51-66.

Wodarski, J. S., Pippin, J. A., & Daniels, M. (1988). The effects of graduate social work education on personality, values and interpersonal skills. *Journal of Social Work Education, 24,* 266-277.

Wong, S. E., Woolsey, J. E., & Gallegos, E. (1987). Behavioral treatment of chronic psychiatric patients. *Journal of Social Service Research, 10,* 7-35.

Wood, K. M. (1978). Casework effectiveness: A new look at the research evidence. *Social Work, 23,* 437-458.

Yamatani, H. (1982). Gender and salary inequity: Statistical interaction effects. *Social Work Research & Abstracts, 18,* 24-27.

Yamatani, H., Page, M., Koeske, G., Diaz, C., & Maguire, L. (1986). A comparison of extended and traditional Masters of Social Work students: A repeated measures analysis. *Journal of Social Work Education, 22,* 43-51.

Zola, I. K. (1966). Culture and symptoms: An analysis of patients' presenting complaints. *American Sociological Review, 31,* 615-630.

AUTHOR INDEX

SUBJECT INDEX

ABOUT THE AUTHOR

MARY NOMME RUSSELL is Associate Professor of Social Work at the University of British Columbia (UBC) in Vancouver, Canada. She received her social work training at UBC and completed a Ph.D. in Clinical Psychology at Simon Fraser University in Burnaby, British Columbia. Dr. Russell has taught both graduate and undergraduate courses in research at UBC for the last 15 years as well as being an active clinical researcher and practitioner. She has produced numerous research articles on topics such as physical and sexual assault of women, adherence and satisfaction with clinical interventions, and feminist counseling. Her previous publications include a book on feminist counseling skills.